"The... individ... form... influen... coming... ...become transformed by the role, caught up in the process,
and able to perceive images and understand
myths which would have had no meaning before. All this grows from a single moment of
passion, no different from all the other nonreproductive sexual acts that came before it. The
fact is too awesome to be accepted in pragmatic
terms alone. No wonder the responsibility is so
often passed on to the gods."

from *The Father*

———————— ◆ ————————

"A SPLENDID TREATISE ON WHERE WE
HAVE COME FROM, WHERE WE ARE NOW,
AND WHERE WE MIGHT BE HEADED
IN OUR DEFINITION OF FATHERHOOD...
PROVIDES MEANINGFUL IMAGES
FOR INNOVATIVE PARENTING"
David Mandel, M.D.

"A RICH TROVE OF METAPHORS,
BOTH PERSONAL AND GENERIC,
DESCRIBING THE SUBTLE EVOLUTION
OF MEN INTO COMPLETE PEOPLE"
Kyle D. Pruett, M.D.

"UNUSUALLY HELPFUL...
SENSITIVE, CARING AND THOUGHTFUL"
*Marshall H. Klaus, Director of Academic Affairs,
Children's Hospital Medical Center at Northern California*

THE

FATHER

**ARTHUR D. COLMAN, M.D., &
LIBBY LEE COLMAN, Ph.D.**

AVON BOOKS ◭ NEW YORK

Originally published in 1981 as *Earth Father/Sky Father* by Prentice-Hall.
Reprint Edition with new Preface in 1988 by Chiron Publications. Reproduced with permission of Prentice-Hall.

AVON BOOKS
A division of
The Hearst Corporation
1350 Avenue of the Americas
New York, New York 10019

First Avon Books Printing: May 1993

AVON TRADEMARK REG. U.S. PAT. OFF. AND IN OTHER COUNTRIES, MARCA
REGISTRADA, HECHO EN U.S.A.

Printed in the U.S.A.

OPM   10 9 8 7 6 5 4 3 2 1

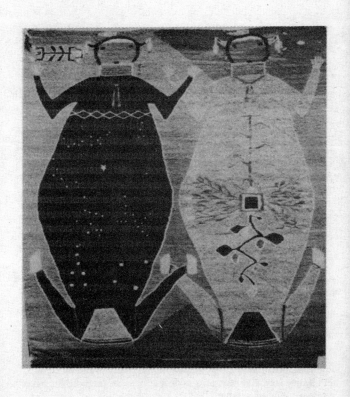

Contents

Illustrations

Acknowledgments

We wish to thank the fifteen men whom we interviewed specifically for this book. They freely shared their thoughts and feelings about being fathers and sons with us. These encounters and the less focused but equally important material from our patients and our students at the University of California Medical Center, the New College of California at San Francisco, and the California School of Professional Psychology have been central to our formulations throughout our work.

We also want to thank those individuals who have read this work in manuscript form at various stages. They include Grace Bechtold, Linda Blachman, Jack and Miriam Colman, Arthur Diekman, Alan Gurwitt, Sheldon Kopp, Donald Sandner, Stephen Shoen, and Stephen Vincent. Their criticism has enriched our concepts and our presentation.

In our search for appropriate illustrative material, we were helped most graciously by Frank A. Norick, principal anthropologist at the Lowie Museum of Anthropology at the University of California at Berkeley; Clarence F. Shangraw, senior curator at the Asian Art Museum of San Francisco; and David Taub of the Yemassee Primate Center, Yemassee, South Carolina.

Finally, we wish to thank our children for making our experience as parents meaningful and for motivating us to write this book.

Preface

In the past 25 years, the psychological and even the biological relationships between men and women have developed in extraordinary and unprecedented ways, evoking richly varied, unique and expanded potentials for individuals and couples. As students of the psychology of pregnancy and the psychology of fathering, we have watched these transformations with great interest.

In 1970 we wrote a book entitled *Pregnancy: The Psychological Experience* in which we explored the changes in consciousness that occur during and after pregnancy for both men and women. Very few other books about pregnancy were on the market at that time; childbirth education was just becoming accepted as part of obstetrical care. Now psychological preparation is part of many prenatal educational programs. Men are encouraged to attend preparation classes and coach or comfort their wives at the birth. Hospitals compete for customers by advertising attractive suites with double beds, wallpaper, rocking chairs, curtains, all the comforts of home plus the hidden back-up of medical staff and equipment. Hospital architects are designing for the needs of fathers as well as mothers and babies.

Changes in the psychology of fathering, fostered in part by changes in pregnancy psychology, have been as dramatic as changes in attitudes toward childbirth. In the first edition of this book, entitled *Earth Father/Sky Father: The Changing Concept of Fathering* and published in 1981, we were concerned with the impact of changing social values in the family and the work world on men's lives as fathers and husbands. We saw immense pressure to change but few appropriate molds to shape the emerging *prima materia*. In the seventies, many women expressed resentment of the isolated life of the earth mother, embodiment of the "feminine mystique." A new generation of women established themselves in the work world in unprecedented numbers. Simultaneously, men questioned the traditional male sky roles of providing and protecting. They sought to achieve a more nurturant, involved place in the family and still remain men in the image of their forefathers. In our first introduction we summarized the dilemma: "the behavior of fathers is under attack, but the concept of 'father' has remained relatively stable. Men who become nurturant in the family often feel that they are 'mothering' rather than 'fathering.' It is difficult for a man to feel like a gentle, caring parent and like a man at the same time."

In our book we seek to provide images for these men, archetypes and myths which would show the way toward acknowledging the father as a potent nurturer within his family as well as a creative liaison with the world outside.

When we first envisioned *Earth Father/Sky Father,* the idea of the earth father felt revolutionary, even utopian. That is still true, although the world of families has changed more than we could have imagined, and primarily in directions that support the renewed archetype of the earth father. We see the changes all around us. There has been a proliferation of books, from technical to popular, even one for children called *My Daddy Takes Care of Me,* by Patricia Quinlan. There is a plethora of excellent research by psychologists and social scientists on fathers and fathering. Bill Cosby's runaway bestseller, *Fatherhood,* while still emphasizing traditional paternal values, is remarkable for its integration of warmth, humor, and love into a usually cold, aloof, and competitive sky-fathering image. The colder versions of the traditional sky father, including his most extreme version, the absent father, is under attack for contributing to childhood problems such as delinquency and underachievement.

The changes in fathering are both deeper and more real than research vogues or bestsellers. Couples are attempting a new equity in parental involvement, even in the early months of parenting. Fifteen years ago we had to look hard to find subjects who embodied the nurturant earth father and the equity in nurturance that we have called dyadic parenting. Even the idea of a special fathering consciousness was rare. That is no longer the case. Descriptions of the father experience are legion even among "mainstream" men. For example, the book *The Fathers' Book: Shared Experiences,* by Carol Kort and Ronnie Friedland, is made up of true stories by fathers themselves.

In dual career families the father may spend as much time with the children as the wife does. After divorce, he is likely to share custody and to be with his children without the buffering presence of the mother. In California, joint custody is mandatory unless it is demonstrated that it is not a feasible arrangement. In the case of "surrogate mothering" (as in the case of Baby M) the father is the only biological parent in the family that will raise the child. All of these increasingly common situations suggest that the father needs to establish powerful and direct relationships with his children as early as possible. Yes, he has a role as lover and protector for his wife, but he also has a role and an internal identity as father. If this leads to conflict and jealousy in the marriage, it is extremely important that the issues be worked on as early as possible, preferably during the pregnancy itself.

Women do have the biological edge with infants. They have the wombs, they create the milk, they have a great abundance of attachment hormones rushing through their bodies after birth. A man has to love and honor his woman to establish a loving relationship with his child. Sometimes technology facilitates the process, as when a man sees the image of his baby on the screen of a sonogram. An obstetrician in California has created a "Prenatal University" to help both fathers and mothers play with their child while it is still in the womb. He feels it is particularly important for the man to establish a strong relationship with the child so that he will love it and care for it after it is born.

These and similar changes in our legal and medical care are all changes that support the integration of a nurturant father into a family system that was historically the woman's province.

When we first wrote about the Earth Father as an image for the nurturant man, we emphasized his positive side, embodied, for example, in that wonderful American folk hero Johnny Appleseed, who scattered his seeds to create apple orchards on the frontier, or the Egyptian god Osiris, who brought the generative waters of the Nile to the desert. But there is another side of the earth father, and he is very dark indeed. In this book he is represented by only one illustration, the engrossing engraving of Satan by William Blake. Satan is the Judeo-Christian earth father, an earth father who lacks any of the positive attributes of his opposite, the sky-dwelling, omniscient Jahweh. Audiences who have heard us lecture rarely recognize Satan as an earth father. It is only when we discuss some of the shadow aspects of other earth fathers like Pan or Dionysius that Satan is experienced as more than simply the absolute and only personification of evil. No wonder the Sky Father has dominated our culture for thousands of years if his polar opposite is so deeply denigrated and despised and so split off from all positive aspects of earth fathering.

This past fifteen years has taught us that the dark side of the earth father cannot be ignored. Once men recognize their own potential for the positive sides of nurturance, they (and their women too) must wrestle with the shadow parts as well.

Nurturance in a man is still sometimes seen as perverse. When the Earth Father archetype enters real male flesh and blood, fusion and confusion between nurturance and sexuality may become very real indeed. Sexual abuse is the worst of it. The negative Earth Father has always been associated with death and decay, seduction and covert operations (as in the Garden of Eden). In fact, with the increase of male nurturance in the family has come a simultaneous cultural awareness of incest and other forms of physical and sexual abuse of infants and young children.

It has always been hard to look directly at the ways in which mothers abuse their children. It used to be easier to see and condemn abuse done by fathers. Women who are threatened by the emergent earth father in their spouse, particularly when he, rather than she, becomes the major nurturant figure for the children, often see sexual seduction in the nurturant caresses of an estranged spouse. Some of these accusations are based on rage and jealousy when a court orders joint custody despite her predominant role in earth parenting in the child's past. Others are grounded in fact when a man without adequate background in intimacy or impulse control is suddenly thrown into close contact with and total responsibility for his needy and dependent offspring.

Inappropriate sexuality is not the only perversity of the earth father. Misplaced aggression is as frequent and disturbing. Inexperienced fathers who care for a helpless and voraciously dependent child may be visited by frightening memories from their own unappeased infantile demands. Girls learn, through modeling and identification with their mothers, to deal with such primitive impulses; until this most recent generation, boys had no similar experience with intimately involved fathers. Child abuse is truly a practice worthy of our earth father, Satan, himself. Still, integration of this demonic side of nurturance is not an impossible task. We have seen several newly married men who have come to therapy or analysis because of feeling such aggressive impulses toward unborn children as they *imagined* caring equally for their child in a dual career family. Often they themselves were abused by their mothers and do not want to perpetuate the cycle as they take on some of her negative nurturant behaviors. We have been impressed with the ability of some of these men to reach their unconscious feelings, address their fears, and proceed to transform themselves into sensitive and nurturant fathers and men.

The revolution in fathering is just beginning. The new images and behaviors described in this book seem to us even more important now that the dramatic changes in family structure are truly under way. But the real message of this book goes beyond fathering and parenting practices. At its heart is our belief in relationship between man and woman, husband

and wife, father and mother, any two people committed to each other and to their child as a profound *way* of spiritual growth. One of the goals of this book is to provide men and women with a more fully integrated and harmonious vision of a relationship which includes committing to and caring for an "other." The risk of such family commitments is not just to oneself, or for that matter to one's partner. The risk is also to the real life produced through that commitment. The risk and the benefit is to the child, the one inside ourselves as well as the one alive in the outside world.

We appreciate the chance to bring this book to a new group of mothers and fathers and their sons and daughters.

THE
FATHER

1

Introduction: Images of Parents

Fathers tend to play their family role through their work and their social responsibilities rather than through direct care for their children. For many families, now and in the past, having a successful father has meant having a man who can earn enough money to provide for the family's needs. He is his family's link with the outside world and the model for his sons, who are expected to move out of the family to become protectors and providers for their own families when they are adults. Mothers stay inside the family to raise and nurture the children.

Recently, some of the stereotypes of sex role behavior within the family have been disrupted (or at least challenged) by new social values. The focus of social change has been largely on women. Much less has been said about the impact of these changes on men, and yet fathers are being asked (or sometimes forced) to act and to feel in ways that are revolutionary. This can be confusing, even for men who want to take a nontraditional role in their families. The *behavior* of fathers is under attack, but the *concept* of "father" has remained relatively stable. Men who become nurturant in the family often feel that they are "mothering" rather than "fathering." It is difficult for them to feel like a gentle, caring parent and like a man at the same time.

Fathers and families need new images of what a father can be, images that go beyond the idea of father as outsider, father as provider, or father as intruder in the home. There is a need for images that acknowledge father as a potent nurturant force within the family as well as a creative liaison with the world outside the family.

Where can we find such images?

Starting from our own experience as children and as adults, we sensed that parenting was a deeply personal issue. It seemed to have as much to do with our pasts and our futures as with the day-to-day present of living with children. We felt that our parenting was related to our personal images of what a father and a mother should be. It was also related to the things that we remembered (or could not quite remember) about our own parents. It seemed to draw from the things we got from them and also from the things that we did *not* get but wished for from them. When we looked at our own children, we remembered ourselves as children. When we looked at our selves, we remembered our own parents as they were in our childhood.

We decided to interview others, especially men, who were deeply involved in fathering and eager to explore the source and meaning of their experience as men. We chose fifteen who spanned different races, ages (the youngest was twenty, the oldest eighty-six), and economic and social status, but we made no attempt to collect a random group of fathers. Rather, we were interested in learning as much as we could from men who took fathering seriously and were willing to talk about it in depth.

Next, we turned to our patients for whom fathering was an important issue. Their stories and their interpretations of their experiences provided another level of depth, for we often had the privilege of being close to their lives for an extended period of time and could trace the shifts in the meaning of fathering through a period of profound growth for the individual.

Although we talked with real people about the meaning of fathering in their own lives, we also turned to books and theories. We read mythology, anthropology, and literature for images of the father in our culture and others. We collected stories and anecdotes and struggled with current theories of family and group life as presented by sociologists and psychologists.

These were our sources. They eventually led us to define two functional extremes in parenting. At first, we called these two aspects of parenting the ''process'' and ''boundary'' positions (following the terminology of Tavistock Group Relations Theory).[1] We conceptualized the mother as generally taking care of the family process, that is, of the emotional and intimate functions inside the group, and the father as generally taking care of the family boundary, that is, of defining its identity and protecting its well-being in relation to the larger society. But these terms seemed cold and flat when we related them to the powerful myths and moving personal tales that we were hearing. The more we studied, the more convinced we became that we could use the mythological separation between earth and sky to refer to the two aspects of parenting we wanted to explore.

The concept of earth and sky parenting underlies most of the ideas presented in this book. We took the terms from myths in which the union of the earth mother and the sky father creates the world and its inhabitants. In Greek mythology, Cronus and Zeus are sky fathers, and their mates Gaea and Rhea are earth mothers. In Chinese cosmology, Yang represents sky and is firm, bright, cerebral, and masculine, whereas Yin represents earth and is yielding, dark, emotional, and feminine. Yet, as we shall see in the forthcoming chapters, there are also gods who represent the earth and goddesses who represent the sky. There are earth fathers and sky mothers as well as sky fathers and earth mothers.

For example, the ancient Egyptians had a legendary pair named Nut and Geb. Nut, a female, was the sky; Geb, a male, was the earth. Before the world was created, Nut and Geb copulated, but the sun god Ra was angered by this and ordered the air god Shu to come between them. Then Nut (the female)

---

[1] In this theory, based on the work of A. Kenneth Rice and Wilfred Bion, pursuance of the work of any group, the group task, depends on two modes of function: monitoring the group's two-way relationship with the outside world, the group's boundary, and maintenance of the internal homeostasis among its members, the group's process. The theory, which assumes unconscious determinants operating in both boundary and process functioning, can be readily adapted to the family system, since families operate as small groups with intimate relationships among the members and within the larger societal framework. (See Arthur D. Colman and W. Harold Bexton, Editors, *The Group Relations Reader*. Sausalito, California: The A. K. Rice Institute Press, 1975.)

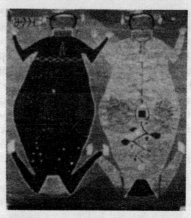

Figure 1. Navaho Earth Mother and Sky Father. This tapestry from the Wheelwright Museum of the American Indian represents Mother Earth and Father Sky as they appear in sand paintings used in the male shooting-chant healing ritual. Father Sky has a tail the color of Mother Earth's body, while Mother Earth's tail is the color of Father Sky's body. This and other symbolic joinings between the two suggest the fruitful interchange between male and female as perceived by the Navaho world view. (Reproduced by permission of the Wheelwright Museum of the American Indian, Santa Fe, New Mexico. Herbert Lotz Photography.)

became the arching sky and Geb (the male), the recumbent, fertile earth.

Whether male or female, the earth parent is concerned with all the functions taking place inside the family boundary, including the intimate, nurturant activities that are part of day-to-day child rearing. The sky parent, in contrast, is concerned with that which is taking place at the intersection of the family's boundary with the community, the protecting and providing functions that are essential for the family's survival.

In our society, the mother is usually the earth parent and the father is usually the sky parent, but in theory, at least, either parent could fill one or even both functions. The father could be the earth parent and the mother the sky parent, both parents could share both functions, or one parent could do it all. Obviously, each of these alternatives would have effects on the development of the children and the development of the parents. Optimally, the two parents could choose to divide up earth and sky functions in the family in a way that was best suited to their personal needs and their competencies rather than passively accept a role in the family imposed by their sexual anatomy and social history.

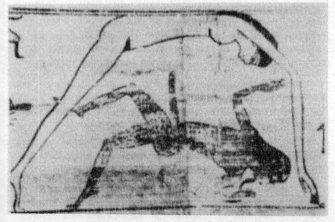

Figure 2. Nut and Geb (Sky Mother and Earth Father). Geb, the potent Earth God, is complemented by his twin sister Nut, the Goddess of the Night Sky. They are among the earliest creator pairs in Egyptian cosmology. This picture is from the ancient Egyptian papyrus of Tamenin. (Reproduced by permission of the Trustees of the British Museum. Photographed by Michael Holford.)

We use the images of *earth father* and *sky father* throughout the book to represent the two sides of the paternal archetype,[2] the most important polarities in paternal functioning. To these two basic images we have added three others: *creator,* an image that attempts to capture that part of fathering which uniquely experiences the life-creating process; *royal father,* an image that combines both sky and earth functions in one person; and *dyadic parents,* an image of two parents who share and combine both earth and sky functions.

The five fundamental images of fathering presented in this book are not pragmatic descriptions of how to relate to children. They are vessels an individual can fill with his personal experience to add shape and meaning to what he or she is doing as a parent. Without such images, parenting can be little more than a chore, a drain, or a distraction from personal goals. When a man senses himself in touch with a larger vision of fatherhood, he can reach out toward a heightened consciousness of himself, toward a true peak experience, even while performing the practical daily tasks his children require.

We offer these images to fathers and mothers willing to explore the breadth and depth of the parenting experience.

---

[2]The word *archetype,* derived from the Greek root *arch,* meaning chief or preeminent, was initially used in Platonic philosophy to describe ideal forms thought to be present in the divine mind, independent of the particularities of everyday life. Carl Jung, who used the concept of archetype extensively in his psychology, defines archetypes as "inherited tendencies of the human mind to form representations of mythological motifs" (*The Collected Works of C. G. Jung,* 20 vols. Princeton, New Jersey: The Princeton University Press, 1957–79, 18:228) and, more poetically, as "manifestations of a deeper layer of the unconscious where the primordial images common to humanity lie sleeping" (Ibid., 7:65). We use this word in a similar fashion to indicate deeply rooted unconsciousness patterns which underlie and shape our person and our culture. Thus, the division of the parental image into earth and sky modes, which are so universally found in creation myths, religious imagery, and societal structure as well as personal dreams and fantasies, is a prime example of an archetypal pattern which humans share irrespective of geography or history.

PART I

Archetypes of Father

Each of the archetypes we present in this section is an exaggeration of an actual pattern that might be lived out by a man. The archetypes are taken from myths and legends, plays and novels, dreams and paintings. They clarify images that individuals and cultures have had of fathers. We hope they will also help men understand the images that are open to them as parents.

For each of these archetypes, we are looking specifically at the masculine image, but we realize that they can also be applied (with few alterations) to mothers as well, for the division between earth and sky can transcend the division between masculine and feminine. We have chosen to explore the parental archetypes through the images for men because fathers have so seldom realized that they could devote creative personal energy to working out a meaningful role in the family.

Each man (and woman) must consider what kind of parenting he (or she) really wants to perform. A person who prefers solitary activities may find himself drawn toward the traditional image of the sky father. He may prefer the isolated stance of the outsider. He will leave the earth parenting to others. A man who yearns to participate more directly in family life and to be involved intimately with details of child care will find that he has several choices. He may want to become the only earth parent. This is a highly unconventional choice for a man, but it is nevertheless possible. If he wants to incorporate earth functions but still retain involvement in the sky world as well, a father may choose to be either a royal or a dyadic parent. The royal father assumes complete control of all aspects of family life. He rules supreme. If he has a partner, she is subordinate to his authority. The dyadic father, in contrast, chooses to function in partnership with his wife. He and she strive to remain in perpetual dialogue with each other, as lovers, as partners, and as parents.

The archetypes presented in this section of the book represent five distinct paths. Each individual, male or female, will probably find that one or another will fit most comfortably. It is our hope that these images will help men and women in their day-to-day choices of parenting style and will help provide a sense of value and meaning to the often confusing demands of parenting.

2

Father the Creator

Parenthood begins with creation. The male parent's thrust
quickens life. He unites with a female to create the family
constellation. He then may or may not carve out a unique social
position as a parent. His role as father is assured even if he
fails in all his family roles. To create life is to be a father.

Male creativity is generally identified as more abstract and
idealized than its female counterpart. In myth, the first and
ultimate creative act is frequently ascribed to the male deity
as the father of the universe. The male is considered the point
of origin, the prime mover, the first spark of life, of consciousness, of thought. It is he who brings order to chaos and
impregnates the earth so that it can bear fruit. Afterwards, the
female presides over pregnancy, childbirth, and infancy. Even
in older, polytheistic systems that have a dominant female
goddess of fertility, there is often a male who precedes the
female as creator.

In the Old Testament, it is the patriarchal deity who creates
the world and the first man, Adam. The male begets a male.
The female is derivative, created out of Adam's rib. Then
Jahweh's work as creator was finished. He watched from a
distance as the family of man, led by Eve, erred and was
expelled from the Garden of Eden.

In the New Testament, the male God appears again in his
aspect of creator. As God the Father, He attempts to reestablish
his masculine authority, lost through the original sin, by planting his seed in a mortal woman. He initiates the plan for

9

Figure 3. Elohim Creating Adam. In this color print, William Blake represented the Old Testament God as Creator (1795). Courtesy of the Tate Gallery, London.

redemption; Mary gives birth and Jesus attempts to carry out the scheme. God the Father is creator and judge, but He does not operate directly in the lives of mortals.

Paradoxically, the male thrust of creativity leads away from the family and the experience of fathering, even away from the experience of a relationship with a woman. His shared ability to create life is readily abstracted. The father role becomes a metaphor for his ability to create buildings, cities, art, religion, and government. His role in the creation of a child is identified with other kinds of creativity.

It is difficult to translate a rarefied identification with abstract creator into the commonplace of parenting a child. The actual role of father can get in the way of a man's other creative moments. Why should a man take on the responsibility and commitment that fatherhood demands? Why work to pay for the diaper service instead of new skis? Why listen to screams and chatter instead of music and the crackling of a fire? In more general terms, why give up individual goals for group needs? Why be engrossed in the process of a small unit rather than an entire community? Why accept limited authority rather than strive for something more absolute?

These and an endless series of similar questions have particular significance now that we have the technology to choose whether to have children at all. However, the conflict between species creativity as father and man's individual need to achieve by himself is age-old.

An ancient parable from India tells of a great Hindu sage called Saubhari, who devoted his life solely to the higher spiritual virtues outside the affairs and desires of men.[1] For his place of isolation he had chosen a body of water in which he had been immersed and meditating for many years. Unexpectedly, he was diverted from his spiritual labors by an old fish who was totally involved in play with his many descendants. Saubhari resolved to partake of these pleasures himself, "making merry among my children."

He went in search of a wife, and approached a king who had fifty beautiful daughters. The sage succeeded in captivating all fifty of these daughters by a marvelous illusion through which he seemed incomparably beautiful. The father consented to his marrying them all. The sage then built fifty castles in the forest and settled down to the business of creating and shaping his children.

The fifty wives bore fifty sons. The sage focused entirely on each new development in the growth of his children and eagerly awaited the pleasure of having grandchildren. He identified totally with the great-great-great-grandfather fish he had seen in the lake. However, Saubhari perceived that he was becoming more involved in his anticipation of the future than in the process of parenting in the present. He thought to himself:

"What a fool. There is no end to my desires. Even though for ten thousand years or a hundred thousand years all

[1]Excerpts from *The Masks of God* by Joseph Campbell, copyright © 1968 by Joseph Campbell, are reprinted by permission of Viking Penguin Inc. and Russell & Volkening, Inc.

that I wish should come to pass, there would still be new wishes springing to my mind. For I now have seen my infants walk, beheld their youth, manhood, marriage, and progeny, yet expectations still arise and my soul yearns to behold the progeny of their progeny. As soon as I see those, a new wish will arise, and when that is accomplished, how am I to prevent the birth of still further desires?"

The sage had been tempted by the illusion of fatherhood and its promise of immortality. It is an illusion because he cannot transcend the yearning for more of the future, for more fatherhood, for more life-cycle rituals, for more involvement in the processes of life creation. So, like Buddha, who is said to have left his wife almost immediately after the birth of his first son, and like countless fathers who (in spirit if not in substance) leave their families and their fathering roles in order to pursue their own "higher" purposes, Saubhari abandoned his children and went to the forest where he practiced the observance prescribed to rid oneself of worldly attachments. He once again attained the condition which knows no change and is not subject to the vicissitudes of birth and death.

The ending of this parable suggests that the path of the saint, oriented away from life processes, attachments, and relationships, is preferable to the illusion of meaning to be derived from fathering. It is a variation of many such parables in other spiritual disciplines which emphasize the individual's need to cut himself off from his surroundings and his relations in order to gain an ecstatic state. Usually the temptations are sex, wealth, or power; it is perhaps strange to see parenting listed among the other seductions. But life creation and fathering are enticements that deepen with time, that may not reach satiation or fade with bodily failure. On the contrary, as Saubhari pointed out, the engrossment increases as the appetite for immortality is whetted. "I now shall exert myself for the rescue of my soul." He had to pull himself away before he was caught up in the never-ending spiral, before he was lost in the matrix of family life.

The parable of Saubhari epitomizes the experience of men who become fathers only to find that it limits rather than expands the individual, creative parts of themselves. Saubhari returned to meditation, ostensibly unaffected by his sojourn as a father-creator. We doubt that his meditations could ever really be undisturbed, for the fact of having created life is not easily forgotten. Even men who, by choice or circumstance, withdraw themselves from their families, even those who leave their mates during pregnancy, are never really free from the image of the father in themselves.

There is meaning in the creation of a new life that transcends the caring part of the parenting function. It is not rational or obvious that this should be so, but then there is much about the identity of "father" that is best understood by digging deep into the unconscious structure of both men and society. Whether or not the creator-father continues as parent in deed, his part in the creation of a new life signifies an elemental reality which no legal, social, or medical act (such as abortion) can truly alter. We feel that becoming a father can be life-changing all by itself, even if the child is killed or dies in utero, even if the overt parenting responsibility is denied. It is the biological act which sets in motion the forces that will in time alter consciousness, self-perception, and even attitude toward the outside world. The importance of the biological "blood" tie in the father's experience is as uncanny as it is powerful.

No matter how it is carried forth from the moment of conception, fathering is still the prototypic creative act for a man. By becoming a father, a man activates his potential to create and shape a new life. Aristotle said that the most natural act for living beings was to produce other beings like themselves and thereby to participate in the eternal and the divine. Plato also referred to parenthood as a means to immortality. Great poets, composers, painters, and scientists through the ages create works that they hope will "live" beyond their own lives.[2] James Joyce pointed out Shakespeare's relationship to paternity: "When Shakespeare wrote *Hamlet* he was not the father of his own son merely, but, being no more a son, he was and felt himself the father of all his race, the father of his own grandfather, the father of his unborn grandson."[3] Thus are fatherhood and creativity linked.

The father's creative act is at the deepest, most unconscious level, impelled by this same impulse toward immortality, although it is rarely as obvious as in the soul of an artist. The decision to become a father may not be approached with the same consideration as the choice of a creative profession or the decision to produce a particular book or statue. Nevertheless, many men *do* understand what is at stake. Rulers whose sole obsession is to have offspring, particularly a son, have been willing to divorce a loved woman, plunder an enemy's land and kill his children, take any risks to insure an heir and a lineage—they understood these issues very well. Sometimes, they, like the fictitious inventor Dr. Frankenstein, whose genius created the engines of his own destruction, are also destroyed

---

[2]Shakespeare dealt extensively with the theme of immortality in his sonnets. In Sonnet 17, he compared the relative value of his poetry and of a child in immortalizing his beloved. In some of the other sonnets, either the child or the poetry holds greater weight; in this one, they hold equal balance in keeping the beloved's beauty alive:

Who will believe my verse in time to come
If it were fill'd with your most high desserts?
Though yet, heaven knows, it is but as a tomb
Which hides your life and shows not half your parts.
If I could write the beauty of your eyes
And in fresh numbers number all your graces,
The age to come would say, "This poet lies!
Such heavenly touches ne'er touch'd earthly faces."
So should my papers (yellowed with their age)
Be scorn'd, like old men of less truth than tongue,
And stretched metre of an antique song.
But were some child of yours alive that time,
You should live twice—in it, and in my rhyme.

[3]James Joyce, *Ulysses*. New York: Random House, Inc., 1961, p. 207 and 208. Copyright 1914, 1918 Margaret Caroline Anderson; 1934 Modern Library, Inc., Random House, Inc.; 1942, 1946 Nora Joseph Joyce.

by their offspring, by the very sons and daughters they sired. Father the creator can never control what he creates, and yet he may be driven to try to extend his own achievements past his lifetime through his own offspring.

With the possible exception of a commitment to a romantic love relationship, there is no other adult act that will compromise individual identity, change personal goals, transform self-image, shape ongoing experience, and influence future directions so profoundly as becoming a father. The man will become transformed by the role, caught up in the process and able to perceive images and understand myths which would have had no meaning before. All this grows from a single moment of passion, no different than all the other nonreproductive sexual acts that came before it. As James Joyce wrote, "Fatherhood, in the sense of conscious begetting, is unknown to man. It is a mystical estate, an apostolic succession, from only begetter to only begotten."[4] The fact is too awesome to be accepted in pragmatic terms alone. No wonder the responsibility is so often passed on to the gods.

A man who is aware of the powerful meanings implicit in creation will be deeply moved when he faces the decision of whether or not to become a father. This concern is expressed in a dream by a man in therapy who was facing that choice. Daniel was a forty-year-old, childless sculptor.

The dream began with Daniel climbing a difficult but familiar mountain peak. He had begun the climb with two male friends but had greatly outdistanced them. As he climbed, he was impressed by his skill and tenacity in the face of the difficult rocky face. He was aware of the beauty of the surroundings, the wind in his face, but most of all of the power of his solitary ascent. Finally he finished his climb and stood alone on the crest. He was ready to take off into the air currents, to fly among the soaring peaks and test his own airborne strength with the eagles and hawks that he could see gliding through the air below him. Suddenly he was paralyzed with anxiety, knowing that he had lost the ability to fly and that he was

---

[4]*Ibid.*, p. 207.

terribly frightened of the heights to which he had ascended. Clinging to the rocks around him, he slowly and agonizingly descended the mountain. Finally, half insane with terror, he came to a dense forest. He leaned against the huge root of an overturned redwood tree and some of his composure returned. Then he noted that the branches above him were moving. A small bear cub emerged, followed by several others, then by their mother and father bear. At first Daniel was intrigued, but as the bears came closer, he became frightened again. The large male bear scrambled down the trunk and began chasing Daniel. He ran across the forest floor, fording small rivulets and clambering knee-deep through large streams until he was cornered against a rocky wall. He turned to face the bear, which reared to its full height and towered over him, roaring. Daniel screamed back at the bear, frantically throwing up his fists and waving at the monster. As he did so he noticed that the bear was really a cardboard model. It had no life or dimensions of its own. Here the dream ended.

The symbols were very clear to Daniel. The part of the dream that took place on the forest floor with its dark earth and huge, uprooted trees represented the power of fecundity, procreation, the family. This was not just the female principle, for the bear assumed an immense male presence. Daniel felt that a part of himself, the bear, the part that represented his future fatherhood, was chasing another part of himself, his vulnerable individual consciousness. The two-dimensional, signboard bear represented the fathering role at its most plastic; the ferocious monster was the father at his most compelling and awe-inspiring.

Daniel felt that the first part of the dream portrayed his most creative aspects. Here he was capable of outdistancing his male peers and climbing to great heights using only his own skill and guts. Conquering the rocky slopes also related to his talent and commitment as a sculptor who was able to fashion the elements to his own inner impulses. This was a path he had taken before and knew well. Flying from the summit represented the sexual and ecstatic climax to his personal quest as an artist and a man. The anxiety and the fear of heights represented his fear of inadequacy and incompetence, as well as his fear of loneliness if he chose a way of life that emphasized his individuality. His anxiety in the dream also represented the pain of choosing whether or not to become a father and the fear of giving up either option.

The dream juxtaposes two kinds of creativity. The sky represents the unlimited, solitary, and competitive masculinity that flies with the eagles over the mountain peak; the primeval forest represents the dark, deep, rooted fecundity and its earthy, devouring family. It is not male versus female as much as a comparison of two different kinds of power, two different sources of creative energy, that of the sky father versus that of the earth father. The great bear is as masculine as the eagle, although the potency is expressed in a different way. Daniel is more secure in the solitary, soaring, and unencumbered parts of himself, even though it brings him up against great fear. The ominous figure of the bear seems more alien and disconnected from his self-image. It commands an enormous attraction, but the fear of it ultimately dissolves in disdain.

Above all, the creative power of the father *is* fearful; in Daniel's unconscious mind that power is competitive with his other creative impulses. The fathering potential reaches from his own underworld to pull him from the great heights that he has reached and both prevents him from achieving the soaring fruition of his efforts and provides a place of rest when he comes down from the heights. But he is afraid of the family constellation as well as the realm of the sky. The problem of the father role itself is graphically portrayed in the visage of the family father as ferocious in the chase but only a cardboard character in the final confrontation.

Sky is a traditional male/father symbol, while earth is a traditional female/mother symbol. Superficially Daniel's dream illustrates this polarity, but on a deeper level it points to a basic split within him between two different kinds of creativity. At the most personal level, Daniel's struggle is internal, and the dream points to the need to heal the split between earth and sky.

There is a danger in accepting the earth realm. The dreamer initially feels that the forest is a place where he can find security. However, the symbols of fecundity are intensely female. In his initial encounter with the bear family, he feels that the father bear is a part of that fecund world, but he soon learns that the bear cannot remain powerful for long in that earth world. In their confrontation, the great bear becomes two dimensional; the forest itself is a female place where the male is ultimately perceived as impotent.

The dreamer suggests that fathering is not only potentially in competition with individual creative aspirations, but also forces a confrontation with female creativity. One of the keys to the paradoxical role of the father is that he can never experience the life-creating role as fully as a woman. There is no process that will ever involve his body and mind as totally as becoming a mother will a woman's. Men have used that fact to keep women tied to the maternal role and that role alone because of their profound jealousy of her biological creativity. After procreation, the father must search elsewhere for his potency. He often moves (or is pushed) outside the family in order to continue to feel creative.

In all fields except the biological, man has achieved preeminence as a creator. He has dominated in the arts and sciences and in the design of physical and political structures and even that ultimate female area, the technology of childbirth. Alone and in male groups, he has fashioned society and culture—with the single exception of the family. In that critical institution he rarely competes.

We can find many examples of men who experience envy and even hatred toward women for being excluded from a process as awe-inspiring as the creation of life. Gods and heroes in myths from many cultures have expressed the wish to take over the entire creative process for themselves. In Norse legend, Ymir produced life from his armpits and his feet as he slept.[5] In an Australian creation story, the great father Karora also uses his armpits to produce the entire world without a woman's entering

[5]Ingri and Edgar Darin D'Aulaire, *Norse Gods and Giants*. Garden City, New York: Doubleday, 1967, pp. 12–20.

the picture.[6] In Greek legend, Zeus did not participate in the creation of the world, but he did assume the power to give birth to individual children. Athena stepped full-grown from his forehead. Her half brother Dionysus has only a slightly more conventional beginning: he grew for six months within his mother Semele, but when she died (for daring to view Zeus in his godly form), Zeus took the child, sewed it up in his own thigh, and carried it to term. Pygmalion, a mortal, found a way to bypass the limitations of his male body; he sculpted his ideal woman in clay. These and similar myths describe the androgynous potential of the powerful male god who can duplicate the female pregnancy function when necessary.

Entire systems of psychological thought have been fashioned on the anatomical difference between boys and girls. Although Freud focused on the concept of penis envy as underlying the inferiority of women, a different reading of his work suggests that it is the little boy's *fear* of losing his penis, as he may imagine his sister has, that pushes him toward stereotypically masculine pursuits. Karen Horney, a noted psychoanalyst, suggests that civilization itself is the product of the sublimation of womb envy—that little boys would have preferred to be able to do what women can do, but when they learn they cannot, they have to be content with creativity and power in other realms.[7] The easiest solution for a child who wants desperately to grow a baby but knows he never can is to retreat to the purely masculine realms outside the family and to anticipate a paternal role as sky father, performing functions that do not compete with the woman's biological ability to create and nuture.

A man does not have a womb within his body; he has no comparable creative "inner space" in his physical anatomy. A female contains the physical essence of a creative process. Perhaps it is this disparity that causes even the most creative men to see the external world as their arena and inhibits creative

---

[6]Charles H. Long, *Alpha: The Myths of Creation.* New York: Collier, 1963, pp. 166–70.

[7]Karen Horney, "The Distrust between the Sexes," *Feminine Psychology,* ed. Harold Kelman. New York: W.W. Norton & Co., Inc., 1967, pp. 107–18. (See especially p. 115.)

collaborations with women as equals in their chosen sky fields.

In our living room we have a Balinese wood carving, four feet high, depicting an enormous male god. He is carrying a beautiful maiden on his head. Five male creatures are struggling to climb up his body to reach the maiden and the pitcher of water that she is carrying on her shoulder. These males follow a vaguely Darwinian order; the ones at the bottom, further away from the female figure, look anthropoid; they have coarse fea-

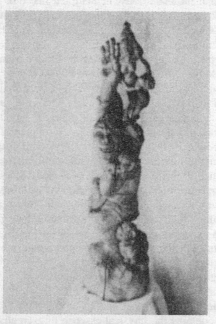

Figure 4. Balinese Statue. Balinese wood-carver W. Pendet portrays man's search for his own creativity. In legend, the true artist must acquire holy water which can only be brought by the pure female spirit. The statue suggests the tension in a creative man in relation to the natural creativity of woman. (From the authors' collection.)

tures and prominent canine teeth. As they ascend, they gain more and more refined human form. The one nearest the top is still less graceful than the female figure, but he has lost the bestial canines. He stretches toward the pitcher of water with longing.

This statue is based on an old Balinese legend about the artist's search for his own creativity. The pitcher contains holy water from a special spring that can only be obtained by a pure young woman. This water, which is the essence of the female spirit, is the necessary ingredient for the true artist, even though the artists themselves are all men. This legend, like Jung's theory of animus and anima, reflects the idea that a man must search for the fundamental element of the female and that it may be contained within himself.[8]

Parenting is the greatest example of male-female collaboration in a creative act. Unlike other kinds of creativity in which the female "spirit" may be needed, here her actual *physical* importance transcends the male's. If a male chooses to express his creativity through fathering children, he faces the subordinate role, at the beginning when biological issues are so important. This partnership may at first feel less fulfilling than other choices to which he might devote himself, either alone or in the company of men. Nevertheless, fatherhood may be his most inspired role. It may also provide a pathway to greater personal integration, depending on how he develops his parenting beyond the involvement as creator.

---

[8]Jung hypothesized that within the unconscious of each person, at what he called the nonpersonal "collective" level, exists a contrasexual archetypal image which may become a balancing source of inspiration and knowledge about the other sex. Thus, within each male resides an unconscious female "anima" and within each female an unconscious male "animus." (See "The Syzygy: Anima and Animus," in *The Collected Works of C. G. Jung*, op. cit., 9:11–22.)

3

Earth Father

A man who has experienced himself as father-creator may choose to develop his fertile, nurturant aspects. He can become an earth parent in the family by continuing to be passionately involved in all that he has created; he can thrive in the center of his family as the prime nurturant parent.

Our culture is more familiar with the image of earth mother than of earth father, and yet the earth father is an ancient image, one that persists in legends, myths, and stories that run counter to the more familiar figures of sky father. Instead of being aloof and omnipotent, the earth father lives in the dark, rich depths of the land. He draws his power from the earth's re-cycling vitality and is connected with the ongoing rebirth of the seasons, with the inevitable cycles of death and birth, and with fertility in plants, animals, and humans. There are many earthy male figures who are protectors of the forest, gods of the woods, streams, and fields.[1]

The earliest and most primitive forms of the earth father

---

[1]John Perry, *Lord of the Four Quarters: Myths of the Royal Father*. New York: Collier, 1966, p. 18. Jungian analyst Perry describes the ancient origins of the archetypal earth father as:

The first Ancestor-Founding King, living in the world of the dead, the earth, or the underworld. This ancestral forebear was divine in a "chthonic" idiom—chthonic referring to the powers that emanate from below. He was the mediator of the vital principles, in keeping with the archaic view that life emerges out of death, newness emerging out of the soil fostered by the dead ancestors within the earth.

Figure 5. Shou-Lao with Attendant, Deer, and Bat. Shou-Lao, Chinese god of longevity, was intimately associated with the generativity of the earth in his role as preserver of life. Here he is shown holding a peach, the symbol of long life, and surrounded by animals and birds of the forest. (Chinese Jade, early Ch'ing Dynasty. Used by permission of the Asian Art Museum of San Francisco, The Avery Brundage Collection.)

identify him with the earth itself. He is the stuff from which life has come. Living things spring forth from his very body, as in the ancient Norse legend of the giant Ymir.

One tradition is that the first man and woman grew out of the left armpit of the giant Ymir, while from his two feet the race of frost giants was engendered. But the giant was slain by three gods, the sons of Bor who was the son

Figure 6. Ymir, a figure from Norse legends, is an example of Father as Creator. Jotuns and trolls emerge from his armpits and feet. After his death, Ymir's body was used to create the earth. (From *Norse Gods and Giants,* Ingri and Edgar Parin D'Aulaire. Copyright © 1967 by Ingri and Edgar Parin D'Aulaire. Reproduced by permission of Doubleday & Company, Inc.)

of Buri, and these three set to work to form the world from Ymir's body. They used his flesh for the soil, his bones for mountains and stones, his hair for vegetation, and his blood for the sea. From the dome of his skull they formed the sky, giving it to four dwarfs to raise high above the earth, while his brains formed the clouds. The race of dwarfs bred like maggots in the body of Ymir, and came out of the hills and rocks when the world was created.[2]

[2] H. R. Ellis Davidson, *Scandinavian Mythology.* New York: Paul Hamlyn, 1969, pp. 77–78. Reproduced by permission of the Hamlyn Publishing Group Limited.

The male figure from whom all life springs is not unique to Scandinavia. Purusha of Vedic India and Pan-Ku of Chinese legend both formed the world from their bodies.

From Australia comes another creation story with an earth father. Karora, like Ymir, gives birth through his armpits.

Karora was thinking, and wishes and desires flashed through his mind. Bandicoots began to come out from his navel and from his armpits. They burst through the sod above and sprang into life.

While he is asleep, something emerges from underneath his armpit in the shape of a bull-roarer. It takes on human form and grows in one night to a full-grown young man: this is his first-born soul.[3]

Karora does not need to take on the more typical sky father roles. He is pure creator and totally nurturant. The myth leaves the sky part of fathering to another personage (also male). When his work as primal creator and parent is completed, Karora, as a true earth father, returns to the earth from which he emerged, to blend with the dark juices of the primeval marsh and find renewal.

Ymir and Karora are earth fathers of the most fundamental kind. They are in and of the earth and are the primal parent. There are more complex earth gods who are also associated with fertility and the earth but who are not the primal creator. Freyr in Norse mythology, Pluto in Roman, Osiris in Egyptian, and Tammuz in Sumerian are all gods of this type. They are all the masculine rulers of the underworld, the land of the dead. As such, they are also associated with seasonal fluctuation and the rebirth of nature in the spring. Through their authority over the dead, they also control the possibility of resurrection and eternal life. Each of these gods is also associated with a goddess of light and fertility. She is often the instrument through which

---

[3]Charles H. Long, *Alpha*. New York: Collier, 1963, pp. 166–70.

Figure 7. Lucifer. The best known chthonic deity in the European heritage, Lucifer (or Satan) represents the darker side of the Earth Father and ruler of the underworld. This medieval woodcut portrays him as devourer and destroyer.

the world of the surface communicates with the world of the dead. Freyr's functions overlap with those of his twin sister Freya, goddess of love and birth as well as the harvest. Pluto fell in love with Persephone and carried her off to the land of the dead. Through her yearly visits to her mother Demeter, she is responsible for the return of spring on schedule. Osiris is associated with Isis, his sister, wife, and lover. It is she who is the instrument of his resurrection and who rules with him in the underworld. Similarly, Tammuz has Inanna as sister and lover.

As rulers of the underworld, Freyr, Pluto, and Osiris are acceptable enough figures to the Western mind. Their relationship to fertility, however, sometimes takes forms that can only be considered pornographic in our society. A male fertility figure is easily recognized by its disproportionately large phallus. Examples of earth fathers with huge erect penises show up all around the world. The Cerne Abbas Giant in Great Britain is a figure cut into the chalk hillside; he is 180 feet long. Maypole dances and other agrarian fertility rites were

Figure 8. Osiris. Osiris was a male fertility deity from Ancient Egypt. He was associated with rebirth of crops and resurrection of the body and spirit. According to the mythology, Osiris was murdered and dismembered but was subsequently reborn. He became god of the underworld. This picture is a detail from the walls of the tomb of Ramses VI.

performed near this giant. It is known that the giant was cleaned every seven years on the eve of May first and that couples slept within the figure as a cure for barrenness.[4] In contrast to the 180-foot giant, a three-inch figure of Freyr was found in Sweden. It shares with the giant a conspicuous erect penis. Similar figures have been found in regions as far apart as Africa and Peru. A picture on the wall of the tomb of Ramses VI in Egypt shows Osiris, whose gigantic penis ejaculates semen into the awaiting hands and mouths of small figures that stand beneath him.

Phallic worship has occurred all around the world, but evidence of it has largely been suppressed in Christian times, especially in societies that have extreme reserve and modesty about exposing male genitals. The phallus is sometimes taken to be a symbol of masculine dominance and power. It does not have to be seen this way. The male sex organ can be thought of as the instrument of fertility and as the symbol of the connection between primal maleness and nurturance. It does not have to imply dominance or submission. The benevolent phallic images point to a truth that has been pushed aside by the dominance of the sky father, that the male as well as the female can be associated with earth, seed, growth, birth, and rebirth.

Some male figures from mythology are earthy without either being creators like Ymir and Karora or being associated with fertility and phallic worship like Freyr and Osiris. These are the gods of forest and stream, the protectors of the flock and the guardians of the field. Some are gods of a garden who tend a sacred tree, sometimes the tree of life, sometimes the world tree. Both Adonis and Jesus are associated with resurrection; the former was born from a myrrh tree and the latter died on a tree in the form of a cross. Sometimes a sacred priest/king tends a tree or an entire garden for the good of his people. Adam was such a caretaker, overseeing the Garden of Eden with its special tree.

Pan in Greece and Faunus in Rome were both shepherds and

---

[4]John Sharkey, *Celtic Mysteries: The Ancient Religion*. London: Avon Books, 1975.

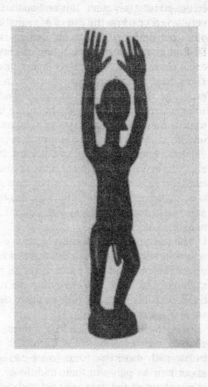

Figures 9 & 10. Fertility Figures. Figures with conspicuous penises and associated with fertility can be found in a wide range of cultures around the world. Fig. 9 is from the Abelan tribe in New Guinea. It is typical of figures used in agricultural ceremonies and male initiation rites. (Used by permission of the Lowie Museum of Anthropology, University of California, Berkeley.) Fig. 10 is a male fertility figure from the Dogons, an African agricultural tribe. Dogon cosmology links this figure with the gods who brought seeds and agricultural techniques to man. The upraised arms are a call for restorative rain. (From the authors' collection.)

forest gods. They were earthy figures who were said to have taught mortals how to care for animals. Bacchus, god of the vine, helped mortals with cultivation as well as winemaking. In Roman mythology, grain was the special charge of Ceres, a goddess, but it was Triptolemus, a man, who carried the knowledge of agriculture to mortals. In Aztec and Mayan legends, the deity in charge of maize was a male.

These earthy figures are not family men, but they are nurturers, masculine figures who concern themselves with the regular care of growing things. Our own not-so-distant past created a legendary figure of this kind. Johnny Appleseed traveled throughout the sparsely settled American frontier planting trees for pioneer families. He partakes of the archetype of the farmer, the chthonic, earthy man, the true earth father who is not often recognized in our culture, but who is present nevertheless.

The various images of earth father are all of clearly masculine men who are involved in nurturance if not specifically in child care. The problem for a real man, as opposed to a god or a mythological hero, is to integrate the participation in generativity with his ongoing life, to carry the role of male creator on into the family.

Earth parenting, by its very nature, must begin while the child is still helpless and unformed, a time when women are biologically more ripe for intimate caring and men still anxious about how to play out their traditional sky roles. It is all too easy for a devoted man to assist and support the mother while she is pregnant and breast-feeding without noticing how rapidly his own role is moving farther and farther from direct contact with his child. Even though he has the best of intentions, he may be relinquishing his commitment to intimate, earthy parenting.

An earth father will want to experience more than the role of caring for his wife. He will want to engage in a direct relationship with the children themselves—a relationship that is truly between them, not one constantly mediated by the mother.

Every man contains the potential for becoming involved in

creative earth functions, but this part of himself may never have been developed in his own childhood and may have been increasingly suppressed as he learned to be a "man" as family and society define that term. If he was ever loved and cared for as an infant, if he ever watched things grow or was close to a pregnant woman or participated in the care of a new infant, or developed a love of making things, or cared for animals during his early years and into his boyhood, then as a man he will have access to his earth functions even if he has never thought of directing them towards his own offspring. Pregnancy in a woman dear to him can trigger unexpected feelings about the desire for a child, *his* child, to love and care for. In the process of becoming a father, and in the interactions in the family after his child is born, he may accept a new image of himself as a parent, the earth father buried within him, and use it to transform his life.

The earth father is a man who interacts with his family on a day-to-day basis. For this to happen, the family (not the community or the work world) must be the man's primary focus. Even when he is away from home, his consciousness will be with his child. At home his activities will be nurturant, focused on the intimate parenting behaviors which sustain relationships within the family. If he is involved outside, it is more to help the family than as an end in itself. Sky functions do not define his role as a father.

To be a true earth parent, nurturance should not be intermittent. All fathers, even the most traditional sky fathers, spend some time playing with their children or caring for their immediate needs. Earth fathering assumes an ongoing commitment which transcends the other fathering patterns. It means that any time there is a choice between doing something outside the home and taking care of a need inside the home, the earth parent will automatically opt to take care of the family rather than participate in the outside activity. An earth parent will take off from work to accompany a child to a doctor's appointment, give up a town meeting to help a child with his or her homework, skip an important business conference to tuck the kids into bed. The earth parent does not always have to be at home, but he has to be ready to go there at a moment's notice. Caring for the people within the family must be his primary task.

Earth father includes the aspect of father as creator, but it goes beyond the initial paternal creativity to ongoing nurturant parenting in the family.

The traditional schism of parenting functions into sky father/earth mother dies hard. The earth father is an anomaly in a culture which is shocked and embarrassed when a man cries. A man who is forced by circumstances rather than by choice to become an earth parent may have trouble feeling proud of the difficult tasks he must perform. He may dichotomize parenting in the traditional fashion even while he is actively involved in breaking that stereotype. His image of self may not include knowing what a baby wants. His outside job affirms his parenthood; working with his squalling baby makes him feel inadequate. The behaviors are there, but the image is missing.

Since fathers don't gestate or lactate, they do not have a biological preparation for their parenting as mothers do. They do go through profound psychological preparation for their fatherhood nevertheless. They, like women, have past experience at nurturing and being nurtured. Their ability to parent goes deeper than a social label; profound attachments between adult males and their offspring do not depend entirely on social sanctions. They exist across cultural lines and can even be seen in subhuman primates.[5] Social circumstances may prevent a biological father from ever caring for his children, but they may also force him to take care of them.

There are millions of fathers who come home after work and play with their kids or put them to bed with a kiss and an occasional story, or take them to a ball game or a picnic on a weekend family day. These men feel that they have close and valuable relationships with their children. They are right. But they are performing as involved sky fathers, not earth fathers, for their major activities and consciousness are directed outside

---

[5]See the discussion of nurturance in male primates in Chapter 10.

the family. The few hours per week are as valuable to them as they are to their children, but this is not the center of their lives. Often these fathers confess to feeling guilty that they are not doing more. They brag about how they walk a child to school every day and then realize that it is only a ten-minute walk, or they talk about how often they go to Little League games and then confess that they missed the last one. Fathers of this kind are often highly valued by their children. It may even seem that the mother's hours of devoted care are unimportant compared to the impact of the father's ten minutes. When the contact is brief but intense, the father becomes a kind of family celebrity, a special person, almost a hero to his children. An earth father rarely gains this privileged position. The earth parent is there every day, taken for granted, unexotic. He is "just around."

If men are going to try to change their relationship to the home and the family, they will risk losing the magic that is conferred on the outsider. The children will have to look elsewhere for romance, and the father will have to learn to respect himself for qualities that may not be traditionally "masculine."

Of all the images of parenting, that of earth father is farthest removed from the values and ambitions instilled in growing boys in America. It may be the hardest image for a man to feel truly enriched by, and yet it represents a most fundamental level of parenting. Rather than being a hero, a disciplinarian, a bridge to the outside world, or a force to be overcome, the earth father takes on the job of providing his children with the basic trust and inner security with which to grow up and out of the family towards independence and a unique identity. For generations, women have accepted the task of providing the unconditional love and care that children require for this fundamental level of emotional development. If fathers are going to enter into the day-to-day process of family life as earth parents, they too will need to accept the idea that giving direct nurturance can be the center of their parenting identity.

4

Sky Father

Images of the sky father have dominated world thought and social structure almost as long as we have recorded the history of our species. The power of the image has been so complete and long-lasting in all fields of human endeavor that, with only a few exceptions, the characteristics of the sky father and those of masculinity have been one and the same. The earth father represents an alternative mode of male function, but it has been buried in our collective unconscious.[1]

Because men have been focusing so completely in the sky realm, the earth functions have become the province of the female, of the earth mother. Our parental archetype is generally a pair. The couple, sky father and earth mother, has impressed itself on our art traditions, our mythology, our religions, our community organization, and, of course, our family structure. We assume the correctness of a strong male leader accompanied by a devoted "girl Friday," a father helped by a mother.

Even though the image of sky father is so pervasive, we

---

[1]Carl Jung distinguishes between a personal and a collective unconscious. The latter is "detached from everything personal, and common to all men." (*Collected Works,* op. cit., 7:66.) Thus the collective unconscious transcends a given individual's personal experience; it refers to things we all unconsciously share with each other rather than what is unique to each of us. In order for material from the collective unconscious to affect our images and behaviors, it must be called forth and supported by the society at large. Until very recently, the sky father image has received this support from the patriarchal culture while the balancing earth father image has receded from our conscious awareness.

Figure 11. Bishamonten. This guardian king is a Japanese painted-wood figure from the Edo period (seventeenth century). He is a typical Sky Father in his role of "Protector of Directions." Here he is depicted with a fierce visage and staff-like weapon, subduing an ugly chthonic monster. (Used by permission of the Asian Art Museum of San Francisco, The Avery Brundage Collection.)

must attempt to define its characteristics. The Lord's Prayer portrays Him in its opening words: "Our Father, who art in Heaven." He is God and dwells in the sky. He is separated from the earth and therefore divorced from the intimate nurturant and fruitful functions. When He intervenes in earthly matters, it is from an aloof position. The prayer goes on to list the sky father's functions: (1) "Give us this day our daily bread,'' (2) ''forgive us our trespasses as we forgive those who trespass against us,'' and (3) ''lead us not into temptation but deliver us from evil.'' These are His attributes: (1) to provide, (2) to judge, and (3) to protect.

The image of the sky father emphasizes those attributes needed to fulfill the protector and provider roles. He is assertive, aggressive, competitive, and warlike. He is interested in techniques, facts, logic, and decision making. He is clear, precise, and focused. He worships light and power. He denies the importance of emotion, feeling, intuition, and the irrational. His nurturance is abstracted from real-life interactions. He leaves the unmeasurable, the uncanny, the fecund, the intimate, and the relational to his earth mother opposite.

The abstract nature of a sky father's relationship with his children does not mean that his involvement is not intense. One of the most moving examples of the power of this bond is apparent in Levy-Bruhl's description of a father from a South American Indian tribe who kept the idea of his newborn child with him at all times, even when the child was in the care of the mother.

> *If he climbed over a tree-trunk, he always placed two little sticks as a sort of bridge for the child's little spirit that always followed him. . . . If he by chance met a jaguar, he did not speed away but courageously advanced on the beast. Verily his child's life depended on it. . . . However badly something bit him, he must scratch very carefully, because his nails could harm the infant.*[2]

Levy-Bruhl says that these behaviors suggest that the father and child ''are so united that what happens to the former reacts upon the latter, as if they formed but one personality, but still more that the child accompanies the father everywhere, and is always close beside him.'' That is the reason for building little bridges and confronting the jaguar. The father must evaluate

---

[2]L. Levy-Bruhl, *The Soul of the Primitive*, trans. Lillian A. Clare. New York: Praeger, 1966, p. 183.

his actions in relation to his newborn. Levy-Bruhl comments, "The fact that he does not see it does not prevent him from believing it to be present. Nevertheless, all this time, the baby is lying in its cradle, in its mother's care."

This tribe imposes upon the man a truth that he might otherwise avoid—the truth that his role as a hunter and defender of his tribe and family, as a protecting and providing sky father, does not separate him from his child. Father and child are affected by each other's existence even when not physically together. This father accepts his child as a very real presence in his life even when he is far away, performing functions that do not seem parental. It is part of his own being that changes his identity and his behavior.

In spite of the sky father's apparent dominance in most cultures, mythology suggests that the male was not always in a position of superiority in the family or the community. The first deities seem to have been fertility goddesses. It has also been suggested that the first societies were matriarchal. One theory states that man was invited to join the family so that women could have a reliable sexual partner who could defend her against rape.[3] The details of male ascendance probably differ in each developing culture, but we do know that at least in the sphere of religion in the Western world, female fertility cults once dominated. The more rational and codified religions of male sky gods gradually took over. Because of their superior musculature and freedom from the childbirth cycle, men made better hunters and better defenders, but they could not compete with the inside, earth roles of the female. That is why the male deity dominated the outside, the sky world. Men created a culture which they could control.

The sky god is Zeus, the ruler of the Greek pantheon, depicted with a thunderbolt in his hand. He is Thor, the Norse thunder god, riding his goat-driven sky chariot and swinging his indomitable hammer, Mjolnir. He is also Ra, the Egyptian sun god; Jahweh, speaking from heaven; and all the other

---

[3]Susan Brownmiller, *Against Our Will: Men, Women, and Rape*. New York: Simon & Schuster, 1975, passim.

deities associated with the sun, thunder, and lightning. A sky god is a protector and lawgiver. He may meddle in the lives of mortals, but only from a distance, for his countenance was too bright for ordinary humans to see. Thus Semele died when she looked on Jove in his true form, and Jahweh hid from his chosen people and revealed himself only to Moses. The following passage from Exodus illustrates the awesome power of the sky god.

> *16 And it came to pass on the third day in the morning, that there were thunders and lightnings and a thick cloud upon the mount, and the voice of the trumpet exceeding loud; so that all the people that was about in the camp trembled.*
> *17 And Moses brought forth the people out of the camp to meet with God; and they stood at the nether part of the mount.*
> *18 And mount Sinai was altogether on a smoke, because the Lord descended upon it in fire; and the smoke thereof ascended as the smoke of a furnace, and the whole mount quaked greatly. . . .*
> *21 And the Lord said unto Moses: Go down, charge the people, lest they break through unto the Lord to gaze, and many of them perish.*[4]

Jahweh dwelt in the sky. He was associated with light and fire, with thunder and lightning, and with law. In this passage just quoted, He was concerned for the safety of His people. He proceeded to give them the Ten Commandments. As lawgiver He stated the rules and expected His "children" to obey. His punishment was harsh but just. He stood in opposition to the forces of darkness, irrationality, and the earth, represented by Satan and operating most seductively through woman and such fertility idols as the golden calf.

In modern America, the male parent is a true sky father. His work is in the world. His identity is that of protector and

---

[4]Exodus 10:16–21.

provider. He spends most of his time away from the family—earning money, serving in the military, developing community structures and services which his children will need. In that outside world, his behavior emphasizes productivity, competition, and aggression. He reveres data and technology and measures progress in terms of growth.

When he crosses the boundary from community to family, the modern sky father enters as an outsider into the earth world, where his values are no longer in force. Here he is expected neither to be the leader nor to supply the nurturant needs of his children. On the contrary, if he attempts to take over the earth roles, he is usually challenged (overtly or covertly) by his wife and children. He may change diapers occasionally or "babysit" one night a week, he may even spend many weekends with the family, but he is not expected to attend to the details of his children's needs all the time. He takes little part in food preparation, hour-to-hour scheduling, doctor's and dentist's appointments, or the quick hugs, kisses, admonitions, and slaps on the rump of earth parenting. He does not deal with emotions. Like his mythic images, he is involved with the larger, more objective issues of the world, not the smaller, subjective concerns of the home. He sets general policies for his brood but does not provide the more pervasive influence in carrying them out. As one sky father told us, "As far as I'm concerned, there's no baby until the food bill goes up."

Such a father lives at the boundary of his family rather than in its heart. When he acts as disciplinarian or decision maker, his influence is dependent on his outer symbols of power rather than his steady presence. His family defines his authority as coming from the outside world. When he is successful there, he is respected (though not necessarily loved); when he fails outside, he fails in his family as well, for his potency is dependent on external success.

The sky father's involvement in the family often manifests itself as concern about the future of his sons (and sometimes his daughters) in the work world. He may worry about their grades, the reputation of their high school or college. He may be concerned about their athletic prowess or the groups they

Figure 12. Thor. Thor, the Norse god of thunder, like many European sky gods, is awesome and distant rather than nurturant and intimate. (From *Norse Gods and Giants* by Ingri and Edgar Parin D'Aulaire. Copyright © 1967 by Ingri and Edgar Parin D'Aulaire. Reproduced by permission of Doubleday & Co., Inc.)

join. His interest in their development is in their status as little men or women rather than as children; he looks forward to the day they will join him in his realm.

The sky father may say he is sacrificing his own time at home in order to improve conditions for his family. Secretly, he may enjoy his long absences, for, at its best, the sky world is an exciting place of business deals, expense accounts, and flashy entertainments. It may also be a lonely world in which meaningful relationships have been sacrificed for material goals. If he doesn't enjoy his work, his family receives the blame for tying him down and making him a slave. In either case, the father can say that he is working "to create a better world for his children."

It might seem as though the sky father would be an unpopular figure in his family. His frequent absences may provoke anger; his excessive authoritarianism may provoke fear. The children may resent his distance. Many children of sky fathers *do* remark on his aloofness, but the sky father can also be a very popular figure. He can be the benevolent one who comes home with his pockets full of candy, who leads the family on exciting outings on weekends, who has wondrous knowledge of the world outside. He is a romantic figure, friendly but unattainable.

The sky father tacitly promises that the child will be brought into the sky kingdom some day. Thus, one of the most important roles of the sky father, ancient and modern, is to provide the bridge between the inside world of the mother and the outside world of the community. This role begins in earliest childhood, when the father, by virtue of his position as outsider and stranger, comes between mother and child to begin the transition from merger to separation and individuality. Some African societies acknowledge this paternal role in ceremony. It is the father who chooses his son's name. He whispers it into the newborn's ear. Neither the mother nor anyone else can hear it. This name is the symbol of the child's selfhood. When he is old enough, he will separate from his mother. He will achieve consciousness, learn his name, and know who he is.

The sky father is like the sun god of myth who brings the light of consciousness into earth realms previously dominated by the mother. He is rarely conscious of the extent to which he separates mother and child by providing an alternate presence in his home. He simply acts out the role that a man must play once he has relinquished the child-rearing responsibilities to the earth mother. *Someone* must help the child leave the nest and find his individuality. From his outsider position, the father is perfectly suited for that function.

As his children grow older, the sky father continues to provide the most potent model for his children's eventual separation from the family. As adolescence approaches, he becomes more and more conscious of their need to be led out of the mother's sphere of influence into the larger world. In this role of separator, the sky father often provokes rebellion in his children. They resent his intrusion in their lives and feel anger at the role he plays in depriving them of a dependent stance with their mother. He is nevertheless the force and the frame for their rebellion and shapes the direction of their development at this crucial stage.

Male puberty rites ceremonialize the transition from dependence in the home (ruled by earth females) to independence in the male sky world. In mythology as in real life, the son is put to many tests to prove he can make the transition. The longer and more intensely a child has been linked to the earth mother and the less love or respect he has for the sky father, the more difficult it will be for the child to make the break. The covert antagonism between the earth and the sky world may finally erupt into an open fight at this transitional time. A boy who dares to leave may be pursued by the image of a jealous and wrathful mother.

In the *rite de passage* of adolescence, it is almost always the father, the father's male peer groups, or his representative, who guides the child through his trials. This is true in the Jewish bar mitzvah ceremony. It is also present in subcultures in which a father introduces his son to sex by taking him to a prostitute. It occurs when the father takes his son into apprenticeship at his place of business or takes him on a tour of college campuses during the son's last years in high school.

Many of these traditionally male ceremonies are now being performed for women as well as men. Girls are insisting on gaining entry into the sky realm of the father. They are having bat mitzvahs, going on tours of college campuses, and joining their father's labor union or professional group. Girls as well as boys are choosing to enter the sky world, which indicates that these traditional distinctions do not have to remain gender-linked.

A sky father's entry into the family during his children's adolescence may be quite precipitous. One anthropologist has estimated that seventy-five percent of traditional African tribal structures maintain a strict separation of paternal and maternal authority which lasts from conception to puberty.[5] The father literally gives up his children while they are young, in full knowledge that he will reclaim them later. The same phenomenon often occurs in American families, though it is not made as explicit. Even though the father has been present in the home, the children may still be surprised when he suddenly takes an interest in their grades, their social lives, and their plans for the future as they reach adolescence. Why is he intruding after so many years of disinterest and neglect? Even fathers who were totally absent may show up, eager to meet their adolescent children.

Whether or not the sky father is able to help his child accomplish the task of separating from the family will depend on how he and his outside roles are viewed by the children. Because this kind of father has taken the outsider position in his family, he may have been either idealized or denied. In either case, it may be hard for his children suddenly to accept him as a real and available individual with all the flaws and foibles characteristic of real people. It is particularly difficult if the children see the father's sky world as meaningless or, worse, immoral. This happened in many families during the Vietnam War. Successful men found that their sky world and

---

[5]James W. Fernandez, "Filial Piety and Power: Psychosocial Dynamics in the Legends of Shaka and Sundiala," *Scientific Psychoanalysis* 14 (1969):47–60.

community activities were not respected by their children. Because they themselves had defined their authority as dependent on their links to the outside, not on any actual day-to-day relationship with their children as individuals, they lost their authority as parents. When a sky father's links with the outside are weakened or disregarded, he can no longer maintain his children's respect.

The modern sky father may feel he has less ability to command his children's respect because of the bureaucratized and depersonalized work world. When man's work was more clearly connected to protecting and providing for the family, it was easier for him to have positive meaning for his children even when he was unavailable for daily nurturance. The alienation of a man's work from his family ties is certainly one reason why men are searching for new images of fathering. But a man filling a sky role has always found himself in conflict whenever he sought to exert direct authority within the family itself. Our culture is not unique. Sky fathers, however valued because of their outside activities, have never found it easy to accept their powerlessness at home. In the family, the earth mother holds sway. Any attempt to loosen her authority is bound to be met by active (and occasionally violent) resistance.

The struggle between fathers and mothers for their children is part of the extreme polarization that is a structural part of the sky father/earth mother pattern of parenting. It is always a part of the myth structure of cultures where this splitting is in force. For example, a North American Indian legend describes the family constellation of a sky father:

The sun and moon are a great chief and his wife; the stars are their children. The sun eats the children whenever he can catch them. That is why they run out of sight when they see him coming . . . he badly needs their fires to keep himself alive. Not all the sun can be seen from the earth; in actual shape he resembles a lizard. All we see is the sun's belly, burning with concentrated light—the stars he has swallowed. The moon, his wife, sometimes sleeps with him at the center of the earth. More often, though, he is

*cross and drives her forth. Then she comes out in the
night and plays with her children, who sing and dance
as she passes among them. They are happy with her and
she with them. It hurts her feelings when the sun catches
and eats some of their number, though he must. That is
why each month she turns her face and blackens it down
one side, mourning the little ones she has lost.*[6]

This sky father is not so much evil and vindictive as he is
driven by his very role to destroy his family. Only by con-
suming his own children can he stay alive and bring light and
heat to the world. The sky father has outside duties to perform,
responsibilities that go beyond the family. He must perform
his duties even at the price of destroying his children, and
alienating his wife, and turning himself into an irritable and
lonely man. After participating in their conception, he has no
constructive way to relate to his offspring.

This same sky father/earth mother struggle is the very life
blood of both Greek and Biblical legends. Gaea, the original
Greek earth mother, and Uranus, her sky mate, quarreled over
their offspring. Uranus disposed of the children by throwing
them into a dark pit. Gaea saved Cronus, the youngest of the
children, and encouraged him to castrate Uranus with a scythe
which Gaea had made for him. In the next generation, Cronus
swallowed his own offspring to prevent them from destroying
him the way he had destroyed his own father. Nevertheless,
his son Zeus, helped by his wife, Rhea, eventually did kill
him. In the third generation, Zeus was in constant conflict with
his wife Hera. Many legends portray Zeus's struggles for the
loyalty of his children against the constant subterfuge of Hera.
Zeus had himself been raised by his earth mothers; he did not
want to slide back into the awesome power of such women.
He was also jealous of their reproductive capacity. He did not
want to be the "second best" parent, so he tried to produce

---

[6]Alexander Eliot, *Myths*. New York: McGraw-Hill, 1976, p. 94. Copyright
© 1976 by McGraw-Hill Book Co. (UK) Limited, Maidenhead, England. All
rights reserved. Used with the permission of McGraw-Hill Book Company.

children of his own. Athena was the most successful of his self-engendered offspring. She stepped full grown from her father's head. Zeus's fear and resentment of women showed up in his need to seduce, rape, and impregnate both mortal and immortal women.[7]

The patriarchal Biblical stories are also full of grim consequences of the sky father/earth mother split. The male children must enter the sky world of their revered fathers, yet they are raised almost exclusively by their mothers and learn to see their fathers through female eyes.

In the story of Jacob and Esau, the rivalry between male and female authority reaches an extreme. Esau is the first-born of the twin sons and therefore the legal recipient of the father Isaac's birthright. Sarah favors the younger twin, Jacob, and plots with him to fool the aging, blind father. She wins out and thus subverts the sky father principle by instating her favored son as leader for the next generation of the Israelite tribe. Esau is furious and leaves the family forever. His descendants are said to be the Arabs. Thus the consequences of Sarah's subversion of the authority of the sky father, the rivalry between Jews and Arabs, continue to this day.

The modern sky father faces the same potential conflicts as the legendary figures. In choosing to perform outside the home, fathers are not only giving up the role of earth parent as a potentially enriching and pleasing activity in their own lives, but they are also giving over the rearing of the children to someone else, usually their wives. When relationships between the sexes are good, this can be a wonderful and cooperative venture. The sky father can return home to find his family genuinely pleased to see him; he can leave the next day knowing that his wife is raising his children just as he would wish. He also knows that, when the time comes, his sons at least will join him in his own realm.

Unfortunately, rigid sex-role division frequently deteriorates to an atmosphere of envy, competition, and hatred. The sky father is excluded from the nurturant parts within himself; he

---

[7]Philip Slater, *The Glory of Hera*. Boston: Beacon Press, 1968, passim.

is also excluded from intimate knowledge of his children and his wife. The earth mother is denied the freedom to come and go as she wants as well as a sense of companionship with her husband. The marital partners become opponents in a power struggle instead of colleagues in a joint enterprise—and the mother generally has the children on her side. At best she will be like Moon in the Indian legend, loyal and submissive to her husband while hiding both her pleasure and her sorrow from him. At worst she will be like Medea in Greek legend, destroying the children herself because they are her only weapon, her only source of power.

The more extreme the contrast between the woman's world and the man's world, the more dramatic the ceremony that finalizes the old life of childhood and gives birth to the new life of adulthood. Part of becoming a man may be becoming not-a-woman, may be separating out from the female world that has been the boy's environment. The transition is symbolized in the Orthodox Jewish prayer, recited daily, "Thank God I'm not a woman." It is no coincidence that this prayer is stressed in the same culture that has become the prototype for overprotective mothering in childhood and an extremely high sky world achievement ethic in adulthood.

Sky fathers in modern society are in trouble. For the past two hundred years, the father's responsibilities as protector have been increasingly taken over by the state—a state that is headed by a complex network of bureaucrats rather than by a larger father figure, the king, who reinforces the father's own authority through his image. In modern times, it is hard for the father to create a romantic aura for his younger children. His adolescent children are uncertain about what he represents and what he can provide. Technological advances are so rapid that the father is often unequipped to deal with the world into which his children must move. They will not join him; they will leave him behind. The peer group may become the guide and support in the outside while the "old man" is discarded as useless.

Many fathers leave their families rather than become casualties of a role that often seems to demand more than it offers.

They become the multitude of absent fathers about whom the "father-deprived" children build their fantasies. The problem is most stark in the poverty culture, where a man in the house is a financial detriment because of welfare regulations; the state is a better provider than he can be. Robert Coles quotes a man who describes the pain of struggling to be a responsible sky father in a world in which he can barely pay for food:

> *It's no life, trying to pick beans on fifty farms all over the country, and trying to make sure your kids don't die, one after the other.*[8]

Even men who perform adequately feel pressures from a family who see them as the meal ticket and little else. Why should they stay with a boring job just to feed children who will turn on them when they come of age? Failure in the outside world can be blamed on family pressure just as failure within the family can be blamed on the demands of work. This circle of despair is a common problem for men who cling to a magical image of a sky father but are disillusioned by the negativity of their actual experience in the role.

If the sky father is always fraught with struggle, what is the allure of the image? Why have men in every generation chosen to play out their fathering impulses in the external world through their work and their hobbies while severely limiting intimate contact with their own children? If the outcome of this fathering style is so often slanted towards destructive conflict with their children, why don't men change the way they parent? Why, at a time when the sky father's role is so divorced from the social reality through which it developed, are men still so hesitant to share in the earth parenting?

Part of the answer lies in the scarcity of other images for the male parent. Another related answer lies in the way boys are socialized to their male roles and particularly to the fathering role. But there is also the transcendent element of the

[8]Robert Coles, *Uprooted Children: The Early Life of Migrant Farm Workers*. New York: Harper & Row, 1970, p. 65.

sky position which contributes to its power and its universal appeal. There is something about the boundary position, the image of the ruler who can straddle two worlds but belongs to neither, that captures the imagination and makes it worth the struggle and even the inevitable defeat. The sky father lives out the illusion that he can be a parent and still remain free as an individual, destroying and creating worlds as he sees fit. His is the unlimited vision of the hero who refuses to bend for the inevitability of the earth and moon cycles. He feels steady as the sun, rational as Apollo, fearsome as Thor. Like them, he claims freedom from the goddesses of fertility, cyclical movement, and death.

The decline of the sky father has been predicted over and over again by social commentators, yet it remains the basic image for boys growing into adulthood. The sky father also has a long history of attack from his children and his wife, yet he still stands as the primary image of fatherhood. Whatever its problems, the split between earth parent/sky parent (of either sex), is the primal polarity between inside and outside, earth and sky. These polarities correspond to a primitive truth in the developmental psychology of the human species and are as strong within us today as in the past.

Change, both positive and negative, is embedded in the very nature of this dichotomy, for the growing individual moves inexorably away from being nurtured by the earth parent toward the independence of the sky realm. Each generation will threaten to overthrow the previous sky parent—and in each generation the old sky figure will decline as a new one takes his place in an ever-renewing cycle.

The task of integrating outside and family involvement for the sky father has never been easy. Just as the earth father's focus is continually inside the family even as he fulfills a societal role, so the focus of the sky father is continually outside even as he fulfills a family role. It is difficult to achieve a balance between the two. Currently, both sexes seem to have accepted the notion that there is less to be gained in the family than in the more "glamorous" work world. When a man is completely successful in the community, it is difficult for him to reconcile his failures in the family. He may turn more and more to the community that appreciates his leadership and withdraw in confusion from the family he does not understand.

Yet, in order to be successful in his relationship to his family, a sky father must also learn how to cross the boundary between the outside world and the inside world. He need not become central to domestic activities, but he must at least be accepted by his wife and children. He can't be seen as an outsider who thinks he has the right to intrude. He must establish himself as an outsider who is loved and appreciated as "ours."

It is not easy to combine the qualities of a successful working person with the qualities of a successful parent. Neither is it easy to accept work and outside activities as central to fathering, to say that one can be a better parent by being absent. And yet for the majority of men, in our own culture and others, the role of father has been defined by external action. As sky father, man is protector and provider, separator and outsider, leader and culture builder. When he feels nurturant and loving, he may think of himself as "mother," because his image of "father" is so far removed from these qualities.

5

Royal Father

The royal father is one who wants to take on the functions of both earth and sky. He wants to be the total parenting system and take care of both the inner and outer needs of the family. Royal fathers may need to delegate some of the care-taking responsibilities to others, but their helpers are in no way equals. Even if they are married, royal fathers do not treat their wives as true partners in parenting.

The traditional patriarch is an ultimate example of the royal father. His wife may be mother of his children and may even be allowed to perform many earth functions, but she does not actually have any authority over the children or even over her own life. She is little more than a slave or, at best, a functionary. His word is law; she is just one of his many dependents—and may be just one of several wives.

The pattern of total fatherhood, of the royal father, is often accompanied by legends that say the fathers themselves are descended from mythic heroes, from deities who held sway in a sacred kingship. Thus, in some cultures, paternalistic rule is totally omnipotent. The father cannot be overruled, even by God, for he is God, the most powerful authority recognized by his people. As Jungian analyst John Perry has written:

The royal father in history was not only shepherd of the people, but also the center of the realm, a function en-

dowed with a magical or numinous potency concentrating in his person the properties of the masculine principle.[1]

Beneath the king, each family modeled itself after the royal family, yielding to the father's decisions in the home and respecting his right to function freely outside. The wife and children were compelled by duty to maintain his sacrosanct role and to allow him through the boundaries between family and outside with minimal friction.

In ideal form, the royal father is a total entity containing all functions, including those traditionally relegated to the female. The royal father does not seek to mate with an earth goddess who has her own strong female power. Instead, he takes a virgin for his bride. She is valued for being pure and innocent. She has little political education or personal power. She performs all her tasks under his watchful eye. The royal father protects her along with the rest of the family and the kingdom. The protective stance robs her of much of her female potency and influence. It also eliminates any competition for power in the home.

Perhaps the best example of a culture in which the royal father truly held sway is the traditional Chinese society. This society, which lasted for more than 3000 years, was based on the doctrine of filial piety which gave theocratic authority to the royal father's rule. In China, filial piety went far beyond the idea that children should respect their elders, as in the Judeo-Christian commandment, "Honor thy father and thy mother." It became the keystone of all religious, familial, and social doctrines. Instead of worshipping an abstract god or anthropomorphized deities, the traditional Chinese worshiped their ancestors in a family temple. The father was head of the household, a position rarefied by the knowledge that he would someday be enshrined in his turn. Every aspect of life related to the line of respect and authority in the family.

In the Han Dynasty classic, the *Hsiao Ching*, or "Classic of Filial Piety," Confucius expounds the view that "filial piety

---

[1]John Perry, *Lord of the Four Quarters*, op. cit., p. 4.

Figure 13. Siva Longobhav-amurti. This Siva Lingobhav-amurti is an interesting visual symbol of the Royal Father. Standing inside a phallus, emerging through an opening shaped like a vagina, he is accompanied by a winged serpent, representing his affiliation with the sky, and a boar, representing his affiliation with the earth. Carved from granite, this figure is from the Chola Period (thirteenth century). (Used by permission of the Asian Art Museum of San Francisco, The Avery Brundage Collection).

Figure 14. The Patriarch P'Eng. An attendant of Shou-Lao, this figure from Chinese folk iconography is commonplace in shops of San Francisco's Chinatown. Blessed with long life and, as a consequence, nineteen wives and many, many children, he manifests the relationship between immortality and offspring. When we asked a shopkeeper in Chinatown who he was, she said, "Ah, he is lucky man, has five children, see?" To us he represents a combination of power and benevolence as Royal Father to his large family. (From the authors' collection.)

is the basis of virtue and the source of all instruction." The book goes on to state:

Only when I love my father, the father of others, and the father of all men can my humanity really form one body with my father, the father of others, and the fathers of all men. When it truly forms one body with them, then the clear character of filial piety will be manifest.[2]

In this highly abstract concept of humanitarian love, the focus is not on a deity or any living god, but on one's own father, living or dead, and on his ancestors.

Every member of the family had to obey strict rules in relation to the father. A son was not supposed to leave home while his father was alive; neither was he allowed to own land or take up rule.

The royal father was supreme in all respects. The women were controlled as rigidly as the sons. The woman went to live in the husband's family. She was supposed to transfer her filial allegiance to the elders of her husband's family. She had no authority as wife or, if her mother-in-law was alive, as mother. Inheritance and family name passed through the father to the children. Maleness and age, in that order, were the dominating factors in the family hierarchy, a hierarchy which was at the core of the entire social structure.

In China the royal father was the human representative of the great archetypal symbol of the culture, the dragon. This Eastern dragon was very different from its Western cousin. In Christian legends, the dragon is made the personification of evil, an emissary of Satan who battles the good knight in his never-ending quest for truth and justice. The dragon becomes a symbol for the evil, shadowy side of man in a culture which chooses to split good and evil into two distinct images. The Oriental dragon, however, is a unified figure, a "whole god" who embodies both positive and negative parts from both the human and the nonhuman worlds. This dragon's power extends to sky as well as earth, combining both in a single nurturant, protective figure. He controls all creative and destructive forces; he is a master of the rains, of the earthquakes, and of

---

[2]William Theodore de Bary, Wing-tsit Chan, and Burton Watson, compilers, *Sources of Chinese Tradition*. New York: Columbia University Press, 1960, p. 573.

the crops. He can harness and redirect the powers that seek to destroy his subjects. He coils around the community, simultaneously protecting it from assault and assuring fertility. He represents the government (sky) but also fecundity (earth). He is Zeus and the earth goddess combined into one total parent, a true royal father combining underworld and overworld, male and female, in one ultimate protective and tender figure. There are no transcendent functions left for the women under his rule. They become little more than slaves, vessels for the royal father's seed, and accessories for his throne.

The remarkable scope of authority of the traditional Chinese father has some parallel in the Western European fathers of the nineteenth century. One hundred years ago, European and American society operated from a strongly patriarchal bias in which the man held all the power in the family and the law upheld his omnipotence. Social custom proclaimed the ideal woman to be a helpless creature who would ornament the home but not be expected to take responsibility for serious matters. The corsets of the age functioned much like the foot-binding practices of the Chinese patriarchies, to severely restrict the normal functioning of the woman's body. The corset probably also caused fainting fits and mysterious internal ailments. Foot-binding made a woman unable to walk in comfort. Both fashionable practices, adopted with great vanity and pride by well-to-do women, effectively restricted their freedom and their competence.

Belief in the father's total authority over his children was so total in sixteenth- and seventeenth-century Europe that a biological theory was developed to justify his complete possession of his children and minimize the role of the mother in their creation. This was the belief in the *homunculus*, the fully formed little person that was said to live within the father's sperm. The father therefore created the homunculus alone. He simply implanted it within a woman who grew it for him as the earth grew a seed, providing it with a favorable environment, but not contributing any genetic material. The biological mother was considered to be only a vessel, a temporary lodging place for the homunculus, a safe harbor for the man's offspring.

Figures 15 & 16. The Royal Dragons. Compared to the almost exclusively malevolent dragons of Western mythology, Eastern dragons are totipotential creatures whose domain encompasses both earth and sky, like true Royal Parents. They dwell in the clouds, in caves, and in ocean caverns and function as protectors and nurturers in all of these realms. Fig. 15 is an early Chinese pottery dragon from the Eastern Han Dynasty (third to fourth century). It is similar to many primitive earth creatures, but the wing buds suggest its emerging sky aspect. Fig. 16 is a blue porcelain vase from the Ch'ing Dynasty, K'ang Hsi period (1662–1722). The marvelous dragon is shown emerging from the swirling sea and moving skyward. The pearl, displayed on the neck of the vase, symbolizes the longing for spiritual completion. (Both figures used by permission of the Asian Art Museum of San Francisco, The Avery Brundage Collection.)

Thus the father was all-creator, lawgiver, and total authority for the entire family. Any healthy female could provide an adequate place. Her body was hardly her own; it was in the service of the dominant male, producing a crop for him. It should be little wonder, then, that men sought to gain complete control over women's bodies in childbirth, for the child was theirs, not hers.

The traditional American notion that a man's home is his castle implies the role of the royal father. Such a man dominates domestic processes as well as outside activities. If the mother or other women are in charge of the nursery, they are subject to his strict rule. In some cultures, the wives and concubines of the master of the house exist primarily to bear him children. Nannies do the actual child-rearing, for they can easily be fired if they threaten the royal father's authority.

The patriarchs of the Western world have been represented not by the symbol of the dragon but by the persona of God the Father, who in Christian mythology was both the creator and the god of love. The Western patriarch reflected God's image by controlling creativity through his mastery of modern technology. Through machines and medicines he could control earth and sky, assert his own power, and even take charge of his wife's body in childbirth.

The rights of fathers were sustained by both religious and civil authority until very recent times. He was assumed to be the head of the household. He was the one who became custodial parent in case of dissolution of a marriage. If he did not have power of life and death over his wife and children, it was only because laws were implemented by the civil authorities— who generally enforced his will.

Men who assume full control over the rearing of their sons often want to do away with all female influence. The legend of Atilla the Hun epitomizes this situation.[3]

Atilla's birth had been anticipated in a prophecy three generations before his birth. He was to be the long-awaited savior of his people who would lead them to their promised land. His

---

[3]Kate Seredy, *The White Stag*. New York: Viking, 1937.

father, Bendeguz, the leader of the Huns, fell in love with a slave girl. She became the vessel of the savior, but she did not live past Atilla's birth. When she died, Bendeguz took the infant and raised him himself. He never knew the comforts of a nursery, but was reared exclusively in the harsh masculine world of mounted warriors. Thus Atilla was raised to be the ultimate leader for a ravaging, warlike race.

The same pattern has been followed in the intellectual as in the military sphere. John Stuart Mill's life was so completely dominated by his father—who devoted six hours a day to his academic instruction from the earliest years—that he barely mentions his mother in his autobiography. It opens with the words:

> *I was born in London on the 20th of May 1806 and was the eldest son of James Mill, author of* The History of British India.[4]

He was his father's child from his earliest moments. John Stuart Mill was a consummate genius who responded well to his father's tutelage, but he also had a severe breakdown in early adulthood. His royal father did not incorporate the warmth and love of a good earth parent.

Not all fathers, and not all royal fathers, are as harsh as the two we have just discussed. A royal father can be counselor and guide as well as nurturer and protector. Shakespeare's play *The Tempest* is a portrait of a royal father who has raised his child. Prospero has trained his daughter in all the graces and skills expected of a noblewoman of her era. Appropriately, she switches her primary interest from her father to a handsome young man and they all live happily ever after.

The balanced father-daughter love achieved by Prospero and Miranda is not universal. A royal father may be tempted to bend the child to his will. When a father takes complete command of his family, he may want to be loving and nurturant toward his children. The difficulty such a father faces is the

---

[4]John Stuart Mill, *Autobiography*. New York: Liberal Arts Press, 1957, p. 5.

integration of his warm, earthy feelings with his inner sense of what maleness should mean. His children may increase his insecurity by refusing to acknowledge his warmer and gentler aspects or even by criticizing him for being too soft and not "manly" enough. Children are even more profoundly influenced by social stereotypes than adults; they are constantly measuring their own parents against simpler images in the culture and in the media. Tender moments may be resented more than appreciated. The father who wants to be closer to his children may be driven to more traditional limit-setting roles by this reaction.

In contemporary America, women and children do not assume that they are inferior in intelligence, judgment, or competence to fathers. Ethics and religion do not suggest that a man is a god or a king. Most people assume that a father has little to do with the raising of children. No one automatically assumes his supremacy. When we described the image of royal father to one friend, she looked amazed. "Have there ever really been men like that?" she asked. She had never met one.

Patriarchal authority is no longer established and maintained by an unquestioned social order. Nevertheless, the basic archetype of the royal father is still present. There are still men who choose wives they can dominate at home as well as outside. They marry women who are far below their own capability or strength or who are many years younger than themselves. They cling to the role of caretaker.

There is room for only one royal parent in a family. When one parent chooses this style, the other must recede into insignificance or face a battle for possession of the children.

Single parents often become royal parents. Because there is no spouse, they must take on full parental responsibility for earth and sky roles. If they are wealthy, they may hire babysitters, housekeepers, or tutors for specific elements of caring for their children, but these people are in their employ. They are not coparents or equals. Similarly, if a single parent lives with a large, extended family, grandparents may provide food and shelter while aunts and uncles provide further nurturance and play, but the parent generally remains the person responsible for the child and the child will probably be aware of the parent's special authority. When the parent is the only economic and emotional resource for the children, it is inevitable that he or she will be a royal parent.

Under current social conditions, there are more royal mothers than royal fathers, largely because single parents are far more likely to be women than men. It is also true that mothers who work outside the home are more likely to continue to nurture their children than fathers who work outside the home. Perhaps women who become royal parents partake more of the earth mother image. They value their ability to be loving as much as their ability to be controlling and instructional. They are perhaps less likely to play out the role in the extreme fashion of Bendeguz or of James Mill.

More and more men are assuming responsibility for their children when they lose their wives either through death or divorce. They are starting to describe their experiences as royal fathers—their long hours of housekeeping and child care combined with their work and community responsibilities. They do not sound much like the royal fathers of the Victorian era who had a household of servants to handle the practical chores; nevertheless, their role is just as royal in serving their children's total needs for a parent.

The inner experience of the single father is often very positive. As a royal father he can draw from the transcendental potency of the archaic world parent, first creator and total power in the universe. These men can feel like explorers in an ancient territory. The royal parent does not have to compete or bargain. He (or she) is free from the power struggles, squabbles, and outbursts inevitable in working with a partner. He does not have to worry about the other parent's undercutting his word or stealing the love that he feels is rightfully his. The royal father is powerful and important in his family; he may carry this sense of meaning deep inside himself even when he is overwhelmed with the double burdens of work and household.

By accepting parenting as a part of his deepest sense of himself, the royal parent runs the risk of a failure perhaps more painful than any that can come in the world of work. When fatherhood is central to a man's identity, his sense of worth is dependent not only on his own performance, but also on his children's choices. As women have known in every generation, familial love is even less predictable than the stock market. A man cannot control his child the way he can control an employee; he cannot manipulate the quality of offspring the way he could manipulate a commodity on the market. It is in the nature of children to grow up and away from their parents, most particularly from their earth parents. The royal father has traditionally insisted on maintaining firm authority over all his family until his death. The new form of royal father cannot do this. His aloof power is replaced with a far more intimate but also far more ambiguous relationship.

The royal father is an exaggeration and an overstatement, a single figure who combines the polarities of earth and sky, merges the distinctions between male and female, combines power with caring, adventure with security, protection with nurturance. He is both the ultimate lover and the ultimate authority. He is the one whom his children want to please, but he is also the one against whom they must rebel. He must simultaneously take care of his children's needs at home and lead them out into the world. He is the stuff of myths and dreams, filling roles that are as large as human imagination, yet struggling to be real in small-scale, personal ways.

The role of royal parent is incredibly demanding, not only of physical energy, but of psychic energy as well. The single parent (or the paired parent who relegates his partner to dependency) must take on all the complex practical tasks of parenthood, as well as fulfill all the emotional needs and receive all the projections of the children. It seems more than any one person can do—and yet it is being done all the time. The images of the royal parents of the past may not seem directly relevant to the experience of the single parent of today, and yet they may be an inspiration and a help to a person caught up in the job of parenting and in need of an ennobling image of the role.

6

Dyadic Father

A dyadic father, like a royal father, is both earth and sky parent to his children. It is equally important for him to be an intimate nurturer as it is for him to be a protector and provider for his family. Unlike the royal father, however, his aim is to share this totality with a partner. In this vision, which must be shared between two parents, husband and wife are both royal parents. Both want to explore all aspects of the earth and sky realms. Both want to be completely committed to parenting, but also to operate on their own. Dyadic parents choose to work together on the life-long task of parenting in a way they hope will enrich both their separate and their collective identities.

The dictionary definition of the word *dyad* is "a group of two." In the natural sciences, *dyad* indicates a pair in which the whole is functionally more complex than the sum of its two parts; for example, a pair of chromosomes is referred to as a "chromosomal dyad." In the behavioral sciences, a dyad is a two person relationship which forms a new social entity that has different properties than either person contributes individually. The word *dyad* has also been used to label what Martin Buber called an "I-Thou relationship," a relationship in which two individuals reach out to one another in an encounter of unprotected, unashamed openness.[1] In this use it implies a spiritual as well as a social joining. It implies the

[1]Martin Buber, *I and Thou*, trans. Walter Kaufman. New York: Scribner's, 1970.

Figure 17. Shiva and Shakti. This god and goddess from Hindu mythology represent a true union of male and female as equal participants in an ecstatic pair. (From the authors' collection.)

interpenetration of roles and the merging of individual identities of two people who form a profound union.

Dyadic parenting signifies the sharing of earth and sky roles by both partners. In practice this requires that father and mother function interchangeably. The father will need to relinquish the image of himself as sole sky authority and accept many earth functions for himself; the mother will need to relinquish the image of herself as the primary earth authority and will have to maintain many sky functions.

Society has traditionally attempted to keep clear distinctions between male and female roles in the family and in the com-

munity. Dyadic parents will have to resist the deeply pro-
grammed urges to separate into the gender identities so often
expected of them, especially in their family roles.

We believe that parenting can be performed by a unit that
transcends the division of male and female. The dyadic father,
uniting with his female partner, completes her as she completes
him. When either acts in the family, it would be simultaneously
for self and other. They sit together as coequals.

We have discussed how, in traditional family structures of
many cultures, earth functions are assigned to the mother and
sky functions are assigned to the father. Although this is a
wide-spread pattern, it is not necessary to believe that earth
and sky are sex-linked spheres. On the contrary, we have tried
to show that men can call upon deep mythic and biological
bases for accepting an earth father image as their own, just as
women can find legitimacy in the sky mother image. People
cling to the arbitrary gender separations not because they are
absolutes or even functional, but because they are familiar and
secure. But male and female, like earth and sky, dark and light,
hell and heaven, space and time, are polarities that do not have
to be kept in opposition to each other. Rather, they are qualities
on a continuum and can come into conjunction with each other.
Dyadic parents reflect an image of an archetypal male-female
pair in which opposites, including the sex-role differences, are
all contained within a single system.

Our image of dyadic parenting is closely related to the concept of syzygy. Syzygy is a word that has been used in biology,
in mathematics, in astronomy, and in alchemy. It comes from
both Latin and Greek words that mean "yoked," that is, in a
pair joined together.

A syzygy consists of two things not necessarily merged, but
linked, of equal strength, and working together. These two
related things can be either alike or opposite. Thus, in biology
a syzygy is "the conjunction of two organisms without loss of
identity." In astronomy it is "the conjunction or opposition
of two heavenly bodies, a point in the orbit of a body, as the
moon, at which it is in conjunction with or in opposition to

the sun."[2] The ancient alchemists thought that syzygy was one way to achieve their material and spiritual goal of transforming base metal into gold. Alchemy taught that the conjunction (or yoking) of opposites could cause a transformation (fermentation) that would produce a new and more valuable entity. This new entity would be a syzygy, a union. The alchemists relied on many symbols to express their concept. Especially important to them were the united opposites of male and female, king and queen, and sun and moon. A syzygy, then, represents simultaneously the conjunction (the similarities) and the opposition (the differences) of the two things and their potential for creating a new entity through their union.

Dyadic parents are a syzygy. They are equals in power although not necessarily alike. They may represent the "opposites" of male and female, but they share the larger similarity of *parent*. They may be differentiated into earth and sky, permissive and strict, serious and fun, intellectual and emotional, or any other polarities that happen to distinguish the personalities of the two partners, but one is not "more parent" than the other. Both experience their primary importance to the family and carry their family roles as primary in their own sense of themselves. Their actual behavior may shift as individual and family needs shift. Some partners are almost indistinguishable from each other in their parenting styles. Others are more clearly different. The important practical qualities of their partnership are flexibility in shifting roles, cooperation with each other, and, most of all, a shared recognition of parenting as an equally potent image in both their lives.

Psycho-spiritual systems such as Taoism and alchemy, Jungian psychology and the caballa use the metaphor of syzygy to represent an internal synthesis, a marriage of opposites that takes place *within the individual* rather than between two individuals. The opposing figures are discussed as if they were an outside pair to make the internal split within each individual more graphic and believable, but it is a metaphor rather than

---

[2]*The Compact Edition of the Oxford English Dictionary*, Vol. II. London: Oxford University Press, 1971, p. 3214.

a physical reality. The goal of these spiritual systems is to achieve unity within a single person. In her book *Androgyny*, Jungian analyst June Singer examines the meaning of the union of masculine and feminine principles in a single, integrated individual, represented by the androgyn (*andro*, male, plus *gyn*, female).[3] Similarly, Taoists refer to Yin and Yang, and alchemists refer to the divine marriage of Sol and Luna, but they are all seeking internal synthesis and spiritual wholeness, a fusion of opposites within a single person, rather than a union between two individuals.

We are using the concept of syzygy to deepen our understanding of what it means for two individuals to unite as a pair in the task of parenting. The resolution of opposition between two partners is not dissimilar to the process of gaining spiritual wholeness within an individual. An understanding of one may be a necessary component of achieving the other. A person who has accepted masculine and feminine, earth and sky parts of him- or herself will more readily embrace these aspects of his or her partner. Conversely, a person who has learned to operate comfortably in a situation of dyadic parenting may discover that he or she has achieved a fuller balance within his or her own being.

One of the requisites for a dyadic father is the desire to be complete in himself as well as a full partner in a family unit. A dyadic father must also be a royal father capable of responding to both his earth father and sky father images. The dyadic father must be comfortable as both nurturer and provider, yet his task will go beyond this personal, inner synthesis. He must also accept a full relationship with his partner.

It may be more comfortable for a father to care for his children alone than to have to adapt his style to the shifting needs of the other parent. Together the pair must deal with jealousies, inconveniences, and individual problems to make sure that all the necessary parenting gets done. The dyadic father must not only accept himself as earth parent, sky parent, and royal parent, but he must also become aware of his wife

---

[3] June Singer, *Androgyny*. Garden City, New York: Doubleday, 1976, passim.

as all those things and see her as complementary to, rather than competitive with, his own parenting. He must be *mate* as well as parent.

In *The Psychology of the Transference*, Jung captures some of the complexity of the metaphor of syzygy in the divine marriage as it is expressed in an alchemical treatise of the fifteenth century called the *Rosarium*. Jung describes the series of pictures in which a king and queen and their counterpart images of sun and moon encounter each other with increasing intimacy and depth. As the opposites fuse, the qualities of one interpenetrate with the qualities of the other to become a single being. Jung uses these pictures to demonstrate his view of the relationship between psychotherapist and patient, especially the way that the unconscious mental associations of the patient are transferred to the therapist and vice versa. Therapy then becomes a kind of mental union. Jung is also willing to apply the process of union depicted in the *Rosarium* to more natural relationships. In the introduction to *The Psychology of the Transference* he says:

> *The important part played in the history of alchemy by the hierosgamos [sacred marriage] and the mystical marriage and also by the coniunctio [conjunction, union], corresponds to the central significance of the transference in psychotherapy on the one hand and in the field of normal human relationships on the other.*[4]

It is no coincidence that of all his books, this is the one that he dedicates to his wife.

Jung selects a series of pictures from the *Rosarium* to illustrate his treatise. In the first picture, the symbols of the sun and the moon are poised over a fountain of mercury, the place where the transformations will take place. Then comes a series of pictures in which a king and a queen, both dressed in costumes appropriate to their sex, confront each other. The pro-

---

[4]Carl Jung, *The Practice of Psychotherapy*, trans. R. F. C. Hall, in *The Collected Works of C. G. Jung*, op. cit., 16:164–323.

nounced difference in their dress represents their social personalities and roles in the external world, which Jung called their *persona*. Each one presents a two-flowered branch to the other. Their left hands are firmly clasped together. Jung suggests that this left-handed embrace represents the difficult decision to join their dark, unconscious sides in a love that is less known and more mysterious than the ordinary social relationships. The right-handed greeting is a healing symbol which indicates that the gulf between the two figures, whether caused by gender, role, or individual differences, must be transcended before their union can be consummated. The flowering branches in their right hands represent the unconscious other-sex part of each lover, the male part in the female (*animus*) and the female part in the male (*anima*). Jung said that this bisexuality was in each human being. It implies that the opposition represented by contrasting clothing and other symbols of their outer roles are more apparent than real. At the deepest levels, we are all made of the same primal stuff, that which the alchemists called the "prima materia."

The pictures in the *Rosarium* trace the gradual progress of the union between the king and queen. First they remove their clothes and, wearing only their crowns, they face each other and both grasp both branches. In other words, they divest themselves of their superficial gender differences and actively share the symbols of their deeper sexual identity. Next, they immerse themselves in the mercurial bath of transformation. Then they unite sexually (this is the *coniunctio,* the conjunction). From this conjunction, they become united into a two-headed hermaphrodite. It is lying in a tomb, apparently dead. The opposition has been transcended, but only at a terrible cost, the extinction of consciousness which Jung calls the "complete stagnation of psychic life."

The image of the death which comes with total union raises an issue most current in modern relationships and particularly in parenting: Is it possible to remain oneself while becoming united with another, or will the total merger into a love relationship bring about the destruction of the individual ego? How

Figures 18–21. The Alchemy Series. These four plates from a fifteenth century treatise, the *Rosarium,* show the progression of alchemical union. In Figure 18, king and queen (sun and moon) face each other and clasp their left hands together. In Figure 19, they have removed their clothing but are still distinctly separate. In Figure 20, they unite in a pool. Sun and moon are still present as separate entities but will soon disappear. Figure 21 shows the androgyn, the united male and female, lying on the tomb about to be revitalized by the spirit descending from the clouds. Notice the birds coming to life, emerging from the earth. From *The Collected Works of C. G. Jung,* trans. R. F. C. Hull, Bollingen Series XX, Vol. 16: *The Practice of Psychotherapy,* copyright 1954 © 1966 by Princeton University Press. Figures 2, 3, 5, and 9 (which appeared originally in Rosarium philosophorum, secunda pars alchimiae de lapide philosophico) are reproduced by permission. Reprinted by permission of Princeton University Press.

CONIVNCTIO SIVE
Coitus.

O Luna durch mein vmbgeben/ vnd susse mynne/
Wirstu schön/ starck/ vnd gewaltig als ich byn.
O Sol/ du bist vber alle liecht zu erkennen/
So bedarffstu doch mein als der han der hennen.

ARISLEVS IN VISIONE.

Coniunge ergo filium tuum Gabricum dilec-
tiorem tibi in omnibus filijs tuis cum sua sorore
Beya

PHILOSOPHORVM

ANIMÆ IVBILATIO SEV
Ortus seu Sublimatio.

Hie schwingt sich die seele hernyder/
Vnd erquickt den gereinigten leyb wider.

much can be given up to another person without the loss of one's own identity?

Jung talks about the paradox of remaining oneself even while uniting with another in relation to the continuing images of the manuscript. The next pictures show a small child rising out of the united but entombed king-queen. This "divine child" is a symbol of rebirth and the eventual rejuvenation of the united couple. In the final picture, the king and queen have indeed risen in the form of the two-headed hermaphrodite. They show that they can sustain a merged identity without losing their separate consciousnesses.[5]

For Jung, the series of pictures describes the unconscious process between two individuals working together in therapy; it is a metaphor for the dyad as much as for the individual. He apologizes for the abstraction of the alchemical images but says that he could find no other way to conceptualize the essence of what he experiences in psychotherapy. Similarly, we must apologize for invoking obtuse alchemical imagery to describe the dyadic form of parenting, an actuality which can be very practical and very fulfilling. We would have liked to have used a more pragmatic illustration, but we could not find one that would tell the tale. To us, dyadic parenting includes something transforming. Of necessity, it encounters the paradoxical truth that it is indeed possible to remain oneself even while uniting with another.

Once the traditional earth mother/sky father roles are no longer assumed, the parenting relationship is of even greater complexity than the therapy relationships that Jung analyzes. Each dyadic parent will become conscious of his own "flowering branch," the "other sex" within. The dyadic father must appreciate the sky parts of his mate and the earth parts of himself just as the dyadic mother must appreciate the earth parts of her mate and the sky parts of herself. Like the king

_____
[5]Jung indicated that there was an awkwardness in this solution, suggesting a continued unresolution in the paradox of uniting two into one. "Psychologically this means that human wholeness can only be described in antinomies, which is always the case when dealing with a transcendental idea." *Ibid,* p. 314.

and queen, the pair must divest themselves of their gender-distinct roles in order to encounter the other in a personal and archetypal relationship. They must accept the formation of the new unity, even though this may entail the death of the old identity and a rupture with old ways. In the process, they will experience their offspring as a symbol of their own rebirth, for the children represent both the individual parent and the pair, and yet neither of those, for they, too, remain uniquely themselves.

Parents have an external responsibility which transcends their own wishes for development as individuals or as a dyad. They must take care of their children. How they carry out the practical task will be a matter of concern to the society around them and to the child itself. When two individuals become dyadic parents, they will be doing more than forming a spiritual union with each other. Sometimes they make the choice because they believe that society's assignment of conventional paternal and maternal behavior is no longer appropriate to the world in which they live. But when they seek out new roles to enhance their own lives, they are generally aware of the "divine child" as a reality and as a symbol implicit in their relationship. They often want to raise a child in a new image, one more suited to their concept of the human potential. Dyadic parents may simultaneously be reshaping their own lives, the experience of their children, and the future of their society.

Dyadic parenting includes both shared and individual parenting. As sharing parents, both mother and father are present and working (or playing) together with their children. In this situation, the dyadic father would not be entering into the realm of mother and child as an exciting and separating "stranger," for he would already be part homebody himself. Nor would his "work" with the children always be some sex-linked approximation of the outside, sky activities such as carpentry and contact sports. As sky and earth parent he would be an appropriate model for his children in both spheres, cooking as well as carpentry, sewing as well as soccer. At such times of co-parenting, he and his partner would have few, if any, differences in their roles and their authority in the family, except, of course, those things that their unique differences as separate persons add to their parenting.

The dyadic father also has hours alone away from home as a sky parent and alone within the home as an earth parent. During these times, his partner relates to the family in the complementary role. For example, when he works on an outside job, he knows that his wife is available to the children. Similarly, when his wife becomes sky mother, she expects him to be home as earth father. This does not mean that their time must always overlap perfectly. It is the spirit in which both aspects are shared rather than the equality that is important. In many dyadic pairs, one parent will tend more toward the sky realm while the other tends more toward the earth. The balance will be determined by the preferences and capacities of the two parents.

Many parents set aside a time when the father fills in for the mother at home while she does something important outside. This scheduling gives both parents an opportunity to see "how the other half lives," but it is not true dyadic parenting. There is no sense of truly sharing earth and sky, only of visiting for a bit. Each parent is dabbling in the other's sphere; the usual roles are still in force. Parents may feel they have made significant changes, but their children will still talk of their father as "babysitting" for them while mother is taking a break. Only when the parents accept each other as full participants in both spheres will the children (often with some reluctance) begin to experience Daddy and Mommy as parents who participate equally in their total care.

Sharing authority in any important activity is always fraught with competition and difficulty. Sharing parental authority is no exception. It is far easier to maintain a pair in which one individual is subordinated to the other than to become coequals. It is also easier to draw firm lines around separate areas of influence than to have both partners share influence in all realms. It is easy to think of a glorious king, fully royal in his power. It is also easy to think of a powerful queen. It is more difficult to find a pair of true equals, king and queen who rule together and who each represent unquestioned authority.

The pair chosen by the medieval alchemists to represent their ultimate syzygy were Solomon and Sheba. Their romance was intense, passionate, and romantic. He represents the power of the sky, ultimate rationality even in judgment over the most primal emotions. She represents earthy sensuality in her richness and her blackness. A similar pair is represented in tantric yoga by the union of Shiva and Shakti, male and female manifestations whose energies flow together at a moment of transcendent spiritual union. The cabalistic tradition is rich with descriptions of the profound unions between the male and female spirit, as one passage of the Zohar illustrates:

> *The Father and the Mother, since they are found in union all the time, are never hidden or separated from each other, are called "companions"*. . . . *And they find satisfaction in permanent union.*[6]

There are other mythical and ancient historical images of sacred marriages which are long-lasting, for example, those of Emperor Fu-Hsi and Empress Nu-Kua in the Far East and the royal brother and sister pharaohs of ancient Egypt. Generally sacred marriages are both transient and ritualized. They tend to disintegrate when carried to the practical level where actual parenting takes place. The union is profound, but the image still places one partner in the earth and the other in the sky. They represent lovers rather than parents.

When males are fertility gods rather than sky gods, the pairs they form come closer to being suitable images for dyadic parents. The northern European god and goddess Freyr and Freya are perhaps the best example of a fertility pair who rule together equally in a common sphere. They are brother and sister, though assumed in some sources to be lovers. Freyr is the god of plenty at a time when Thor and Odin were the sky gods. Freyr is often pictured with an enormous erect phallus (symbolizing the male power of fruitfulness rather than the

---

[6]This quotation from Zohar III, 77b–78a, is quoted from Raphael Patai, *The Hebrew Goddess*. New York: Avon Books, 1978, p. 137.

weapons of war). Weapons and blood are outlawed on his sacred ground.

Freya, like her brother, rules through fertility cults. She is concerned with peace and prosperity, though perhaps on a more intimate level than he. She is important in matters of love and is the goddess of labor and childbirth. She has magical powers and inspires ecstatic fertility rites. Both Freyr and Freya are concerned with the land of the dead. Unlike many ruling pairs, they share power in the same realm without separating their spheres of influence or creating a hierarchy.

In a more widespread form of fertility pairs, one must die to insure the renewal of the earth. In the stories of such earth fathers as Osiris, Tammuz, Attis, and Adonis, the young male gods are killed and resurrected after sexual union with the goddess as part of a seasonal rite. These stories teach that love is transient and that the power to rule must be invested in one rather than in both equally.

Probably the most stable pairs in myths and legends are those in which male and female do not share authority at all. In the era of matriarchy, when the goddess was preeminent, the male counterpart appeared as a powerless consort, son, or son-lover. These young men were used to satisfy the goddess's sexual and fertility needs but had no authority except through their association with her. Patriarchy reversed the power structure. Women became passive receptacles for masculine potency and progeny. In the developed patriarchal systems, myths reflected more ambivalence between the sexes, although the sky father was still supreme. Zeus and Hera remain together eternally, despite interminable squabbling and infidelity. There is no pretense of equality or shared general authority in their relationship, though they do agree upon spheres of influence which must not be violated. Hera is not satisfied with this arrangement and challenges her husband through sly subterfuge in the same way that Sarah tricked Isaac or that a modern housewife might manipulate her executive husband. These unions last because the male's formal authority is never in question and the female's resentment finds an outlet in day-to-day subversion. These are not the images that would be meaningful to dyadic parents. Rather, they remain apt descriptions of the traditional pairings within our own society in which a modified patriarchy is still the dominant family form.

Our society contains many images of coequal pairs who are young adults. Our media are full of men and women who are paired as lovers and companions. What is missing is the transition to a sharing couple as parents. Something happens to the equality in the relationship when parenthood intervenes. The same couple who have learned to share their bed, board, friends, and work roles seem to change when taking on the responsibility of sharing roles as parents and the pressures to conform to traditional sex-linked roles.

In recent years, economic pressure and sexual politics have changed some of our attitudes toward the traditional family stereotypes. Women are earning better salaries, often equal or superior to that of their husbands, before they have children. It is often possible to retain much of that earning ability by having the husband share in child care and housekeeping. Furthermore, women may not be willing to drop their careers in order to serve the earth goddess exclusively for ten to fifteen years. Men of today may also feel less inclined to devote themselves totally to job and community. Our institutional work structures are more secure but less exciting. Staying at home with the children may have more appeal for men now than it did in the past.

The economic and social forces that have made sharing earth and sky roles more possible and more appealing are slowly changing sex-role expectations. Sky and earth images are no longer rigidly sex-linked, but neither are they distinct from gender. There is still an absence of images for truly shared parenting.

Some of the "changes" that we have been talking about are new to the middle class but not to the rich or to the poor. Among the poor, two jobs have often meant survival when one salary would not pay for food and rent. Among the rich, supplementary care-givers in the form of servants have freed both parents to work or play as they choose. It is only in the past generation that the middle class has been making arrangements which equalize both parents within the family. In this new wave, sometimes called "dual-career families," the pattern is an interesting blend of necessity and luxury. Some of these families could pay the bills with only one salary, although not be able to live as luxuriously as they choose. Probably as important, however, they could not fulfill the psychological and emotional needs of both partners to be both nurturant and successful in the world if they adhered to a rigid split in sex roles. These dual-career couples do very well until they contemplate parenthood. Then the sky father/earth mother stereotype may threaten their equilibrium. Many couples solve the issue by not having children, a decision which now gains more social support than in the past. Most couples, however, do become parents. When they lapse into traditional family patterns, they experience conflict within themselves. When they try to create a workable pattern as true partners, they feel like pioneers in a new form.

If becoming a dyadic parent is not yet entirely supported in our society, neither is it unacceptable. As it becomes a choice for couples starting out in a new relationship, both participants will need to understand the personal implications of sharing in areas which have been separated by sex. The man may face the greater challenge, for he must give up some of the prerogatives that society has placed in highest esteem. The dyadic father must accept a limitation on his career, for he can no longer expect unequivocal support and self-sacrifice from his mate when needs on the job interfere with life at home. He may also need to accept some limitations in his personal time. Men have traditionally used the real but exaggerated difficulty of their work commitments as justification for isolating themselves from their families to do other things—to have a beer with the gang or a drink after hours with a client, or to retreat to the TV or to the den. Dyadic parents must share and compromise. If a man expects marriage to be an intense, ongoing relationship that penetrates all areas of his experience, the constraints will feel like the "work" that achieves this goal.

Some men feel claustrophobic at the idea of sharing everything with a woman. It cannot be denied that children make even more demands than a mate. They impinge on personal freedom and even on the most basic sense of individual identity. To be suited for dyadic parenting, a man should have a fundamental commitment to the value of deep, two-person relationships, yet he must also not be afraid to deal with the threat that the family represents to his primary relationship with his wife.

The dyad that is the love relationship between the parents is altered by the presence of children, each of whom establishes his or her own dyadic relationship with the father. In the complex network that makes up a family, it may be difficult to keep all of the dyads equally alive and meaningful.

A man who chooses to become a sky father can project all his "female" nurturant qualities onto his wife, who is doing the earth parenting for him. The dyadic father must strive towards completeness in himself and must accept the same wish in his partner. He may combine all potential parenting qualities within himself, yet he has a chance to escape from them occasionally because his partner can take over in his absence. She, too, can nurture, protect, and provide. He can do all things part of the time. This image combines the advantages of the earth/sky split with the advantages of the royal parent.

PART II

Images of the Sky Father Through the Life Cycle

The archetypal images of father that we have described in Part One (earth, sky, creator, royal, and dyadic) are abstractions of many possible fathering roles that a man can take in a family. They do not define rigid categories that limit what is possible for an individual. Rather, they are the larger-than-life manifestations of the potential within every father and images of him that might be perceived by every son and daughter.

Before we look at the experience of families which have chosen nontraditional paths, we want to review the traditional meaning of fatherhood through the life cycle. By traditional we mean the experience that has been accepted by male parents as the way to be a father in the family and in the community. This traditional model comes very close to that of the sky father.

The sweep through the life history of fathers in general cannot be inclusive. People are too diverse to be captured in a single profile. Nevertheless, we want to suggest that fathering is a developmental theme that can be traced through any individual's life history. The meaning of "father" shifts for us as we move through our life cycle. We will be influenced by our society's image of what a father should be and by our perception of our own father's person and his ability (or inability) to live up to this ideal. All of us will continue to feel the influence of our fathers on our lives well beyond childhood. We do more than depend on a father's care when we are young; we continue to yearn for his approval and cry out against his shortcomings in our maturity and even in our old age. A father is remembered by his children far beyond his own lifetime and has profound meaning to them up to their own deaths.

In this section of the book, we will explore the unique meaning of traditional sky fathers in the unconscious of their children as well as the meaning of *being* a father to a man in his adulthood. We will begin with the infant's earliest awareness of the male parent as personal consciousness first emerges. Then we will consider the child's and the adolescent's awareness of *father*. We will look at the turning point that occurs when the child first becomes an adult and then becomes a father himself. We will end with the stage of reconciliation in which the grown-up child attempts to perceive his father as a real person as well as a personal representative of an archetype.

7

The Early Father-Child
Relationship: Idealization

How does a father first affect his child? We can only guess an
answer. There are no verbal memories and no developed concepts or images from the earliest period of a child's life. Some
older children and adults can recollect vague sensory impres-
sions, hazy shadows, and inchoate emotions from this period.
No matter how little is remembered, we believe that the pre-
conscious relationship with father has powerful consequences
for development. Indelibly, it shapes all that is to come after.

When we try to understand the emergence of consciousness
in an infant, certain experiences can be assumed. First, there
is the womb. We know that it is dark and at a constant tem-
perature, that it is filled with the sounds of the mother's heart-
beat and her digestive system, that it moves as the mother
moves. We can imagine that the developing fetus can perceive
these qualities, but that it can not distinguish itself from its
surroundings. The fetal brain reacts to sounds and movements;
it may be said to be "conscious," but there is not yet any
conception of "I" nor any perception of parent as a personal
caretaker.

The child is not born instantly into an awareness of its own
individuality and separateness from its parents. "Psychological
birth," the process through which an individual recognizes his
own uniqueness, is far more complicated than physical birth

and takes much longer. A Jungian analyst describes the origins of our individual consciousness and the initial image of parents:

> *This original darkness is called the unconscious today, but in the terms used by many religions it is the* Void, *the condition of nothingness that, it is said, existed before the gods came into being. The gods of our infancy are, of course, represented by the parents, who encompass the babe like the confines of a world, while he lies sleeping within their enclosure, at first as an unborn embryo, and later like a child in a fairy tale world—a personal Garden of Eden. The parents thus form an encircling and protective covering that represents for the individual the maternal and paternal uroboros (world serpent).*[1]

The child emerges gradually into consciousness. The rudimentary process of separation and individuation is thought to require at least three years.[2] In order to complete this task, the child must break the symbiotic bond, its merger with its earth parent. The end-point of this developmental stage is the beginning of a personal identity, an "I," that it can more or less consistently recognize as its own.

In a traditional family, the father often plays his first direct role in the child's development by being an attractive outsider who can draw the child away from its merger state with the mother (generally the sole earth parent) toward a separate individuality. As sky parent, the father is the prototype of the outside world. He stands for separateness, consciousness, and adventure, and his difference from the earth mother's inwardness is an important developmental force.

---

[1] M. Esther Harding, *The Parental Image: Its Injury and Reconstruction*. New York: Putnam's, 1965, p. 25.

[2] Both psychoanalytic and child development theory have contributed to understanding the extent to which a child's individual identity requires a maturational process which is most intense in the first three years of life but which extends into adolescence and adulthood as well. See M. S. Mahler, "Thoughts about Development and Individuation," *The Psychoanalytic Study of the Child* 18 (1963):307–24.

In infancy, then, the father's necessary function is to create a family unit, to stabilize the mother, to balance the mother-child relationship, to relate the psychobiological unit of mother and child to the objective world, and finally to penetrate the infant's world with the potential pleasurable stimulation and interest of the outside world.[3]

We still know very little about the process of early child development when the earth parent is a male or when that role is shared by more than one person. All of the caretakers and their roles in the primary and extended families must influence an infant's developing awareness of the relationship between itself and other.[4] We will speculate on the developmental effects of nontraditional parenting in Chapter 13. For the purposes of this section, we will assume a traditional family in which the mother is the earth parent and the father is the sky parent, for this remains the standard against which other patterns are measured.

A child's earliest awareness of its sky father may be very romantic. As representative of the outside world, he may be aloof, but he can also be seen as heroic. Libby reminisces about her father, who was literally in the sky world as an officer in the United States Air Force:

I was born in March 1940, just before the United States entered World War II. I remember hearing my father say, "It must really have been bad if they were drafting old men like me." At the time I thought he was being modest.

---

[3]Tess Forest, "The Paternal Roots of Character Development," *Psychoanalytic Review* 54 (1961):55.

[4]In another work, *Love and Ecstasy* (New York: Seabury Press, 1975), we hypothesize a stage of group consciousness which lies between total symbiosis with the earth parent(s) and which precedes individual consciousness. In this stage, the child is always discriminating between all those who are "sky"—outside and separated—and all those who are "earth"—inside and merged. Consciousness is always changing, depending on the child's relationship with those present, be they traditional or nontraditional parents, siblings, friends, or strangers. Eventually the child learns to separate himself from the group flux and emerges as someone separate and apart from all others.

Now I realize that he was really shocked and dismayed. He must have been thirty-nine or forty years old at that time. He had three children between the ages of one and five and had just taken a job away from the city in an atmosphere that he considered to be healthy for children. I suppose now that he had planned to settle there and spend the rest of his life as a weekend gardener. Instead, he became a hero (in my eyes anyway) in spite of himself.

I don't remember moving to Washington, but I remember being there. I have a clearer image of Andrews Air Force Base than I do of the inside of our home. I remember the excitement with which I anticipated a trip to the base. When we identified ourselves to the guard at the gate, I felt huge, like a celebrity. My father had an office in there amid all those big airplanes. I knew the planes weren't his, but he became bigger (and I think shinier) because of his association with them. After all, he wore the same insignia on his uniform as they had painted on their fuselages. I have no memories of my father inside our home in those years, although I have distinct memories of him driving the car, walking across the base, and sitting in his office.

I don't remember any pain or anger or sense of loss when he flew overseas. He was in "intelligence," and I was very proud of that. To me it meant that they had drafted him because he was smart. Years after the war was over I clung to the image that my father was "intelligent" and used it to put down other kids in the school yard.

Now that I have lived through the experience of raising three children of school age, I am appalled at how blind I was to my parents' experience. I see photographs of the family during that time. My mother looks strained, even haggard; my older brother was skinny and sickly; my sister wore a very forced smile for the camera; but I look

*radiant. I believe I was really pleased to have my Daddy
go off to war and be such a perfect sky parent.*

Libby is not the only child who has adored a sky father. It
is a glorious image filled with great power. A very young child
may have a rather unrealistic vision of what the father is actually doing in the sky world. We were made aware of this by
watching our son Ari when he was two. Arthur was to go away
for a few days. Ari went to the heliport to see him off. When
Ari saw his father walking towards the noisy, frightening helicopter, he started screaming hysterically. It was quite clear
that he thought Arthur was being consumed by a horrible monster. We consoled him, but he was obviously still troubled.
Fortunately, that same helicopter passed over our house three
times a day on its way from Marin County to the San Francisco
airport. Each time it went by, Ari pointed to it and said,
"Daddy, Daddy." He thought his Daddy was still inside the
helicopter flying around in the sky. We assured him his Daddy
would be coming back, and he ran happily outside three times
a day to watch his sky hero fly past.

Since we have started thinking about the meaning of sky
fathers to their children, we have realized how many pre-
schoolers create wonderful fantasies about where such fathers
go each day and what they do while they are gone.

Many people recall early images of their fathers as godlike
giants. These distant sky figures are always there, yet never
fully within grasp. They seem powerful and special, but also
mysterious. They may become heroes or villains. As the first
stranger, father epitomizes escape from dependence. Even if
there are other outsiders, such as babysitters and siblings and
grandparents, Daddy seems to develop a special aura in the
very young child's consciousness.

Father is a breath of fresh air, an intensely exciting alternative to the too-familiar family that is home with the child
all day. He is likely to be greeted with almost hysterical en-
thusiasm by an adoring toddler who is increasingly ready to
leave his mother's (or other caretaker's) arms and seek adven-

tures elsewhere. The games that develop between father and child tend to be more physical and often more joyful than those with mother, who becomes the security blanket when the risks of play become more frightening than exhilarating. The child is enticed farther and farther away from the maternal orbit in a process that will end many years later in the separation from the family itself.

If the child sees the father as leading the way toward separation, his role brings joy, but also fear. Mother may be smothering, but she is also safe. Dependence may be stifling, but it is also secure. The father may become the favorite parent, but there can be deep resentment accompanying the pleasure. Father is the powerful and benign creator who protects his dependent creatures in paradise, but he is also the serpent who enters from without and who whispers of hidden knowledge and of a world that lies beyond.

As a representative of the outside world and an alternative to the earth mother, the father is at first idealized and made almost omnipotent. Sometimes the child's wish is to erase all memory of the mother in favor of the father. Consider the father figures in favorite fairy tales. Both Cinderella and Snow White are stories of young girls being persecuted by wicked stepmothers. A handsome young prince finally saves each of them. But how did Cinderella and Snow White get into the clutches of these wicked women? We learn that the heroines once had fathers, good men, whose wives had sadly died. The father cannot bring up the child all by himself, so he marries a terrible woman. In most versions he protects the daughter for a while and then dies, leaving Cinderella or Snow White to her stepmother. The fantasy of the father persists in the heroine's mind; *he* would have saved her if he were alive. In reality, of course, he would have done nothing of the kind. In memory, he is golden; in actuality, he himself presented his beloved daughter to the witch.

One of the important elements in these stories is the strain between the fantasy of father as protective parent and his real inability to stave off disaster. In these tales, the father hardly deserves the heroic aura he is given. If his actions are obviously reprehensible, the belief in a male protector is shifted to the handsome young prince, the potential father of the heroine's own generation. The psychological appeal of the myth of the good father transcends the facts of the stories.

While we were working on this chapter, we came across a group of five-year-old boys playing in a park. After a little while, we fell into conversation with them. We took the opportunity to ask their expert opinions on the question, "What are fathers for?" They were very quick to answer that fathers were to "take care of kids." We were a little surprised at that. To these boys nurturance was a father's primary trait! However, they soon qualified their answer to say that he was especially for taking care of *boy* children and that he would take care of them in case of fires and earthquakes—that his caring was more protective than nurturant. We asked what dads do while waiting for a fire or an earthquake. One boy started to say, "If you don't have a mom. . . . " and the others had all nodded while another boy finished the sentence, "yeah, you'd just tell your father." He was perceived as a protective sky parent, but also as a second-string earth parent to be called on if Mom was gone. But they agreed, if you had a mom, "you wouldn't have to tell your dad."

"Do you ever sit on your father's lap?" we asked. One boy said, "I used to when I was little, but I don't anymore because now I weigh fifty pounds." Another boy yelled out, "I love it when he puts me to bed." The others were amazed. "I don't," one remarked. "He says 'get to bed' when I'm playing with my toys. I hate it."

"Do fathers ever get mad?" "Yeah, they sure do." Every boy in the group was sure of that! They get madder than moms. One said his father was *always* right and he got "scared like anything" when his father yelled. Another said he thought his father was wrong a lot. "I feel like he's doing something wrong by yelling." Another was awed. He said his father was "like Spiderman to me." But they agreed it was a father's job to tell them what was right and what was wrong.

A boy spontaneously burst out, "My dad takes me to work sometimes." Suddenly all the boys had something to say. They were vying for the dad that had the most interesting work. The one whose father was a carpenter won. He told about how his dad climbed big ladders to hang shingles and even showed off a proud scar he'd gotten at his father's work. The son of a lawyer couldn't compete. "My Daddy promised me he would show me his office, but he hasn't had time." Two sons of doctors were able to do a little better. They started an argument about whose dad had touched more parts inside the body than the other. These discussions were so intense that it was clear the image of dad at work was as heroic as that of him saving his son from a fire, and far more real.

For these boys the fathers are more adulated than feared, although their intense reactions to his potential wrath show that he represents a rather austere and powerful authority.

Both little boys and girls have trouble understanding that father may not be a hero. For a boy particularly, the unconscious resentment of the strange man who stood between mother and son in early childhood gives way to a powerful identification with the huge male, the man who is so wonderful that mother prefers him and the child feels safe in his masculinity. Every little boy who ever said to his playmate "My dad can beat up your dad" was sure that he was right, sure that his dad would be the winner in any contest. Unfortunately, this overenthusiastic idealizing passes! Even a boy with a strong and admirable father has to grow into a young man who recognizes that his father is real and limited, not ideal and omnipotent. The discovery is often accompanied by fury and contempt, as though the father had in some way betrayed the boy by not remaining a god. In his disillusionment, the son turns against his father, exaggerating his faults and weaknesses. This turnabout is almost always out of proportion to the situation and takes most fathers, so recently worshipped, by surprise. The child moves from idealization to reevaluation of the father, a psychological process which often results in a rejection of and alienation from the recent hero.

8

Coming of Age:
Alienation and Ambivalence

As the child begins to extend its own life outside the family, it gains a new perspective of its father. He is compared to other men—especially to other people's fathers—and to the faint memory of a larger, younger, more heroic man who was the father as he appeared to the very young child. When our daughter Shoshana was eleven, she told us how she had felt at age seven when Arthur's favorite dog was killed by a car. "Until I saw you cry that way, I didn't quite believe you were a real person. I thought you were Thor. Sometimes I still think so, though I know better." Her choice of Thor as her paternal image was affected by a much-read, illustrated book of Norse legends in which Thor was pictured as having a reddish beard very much like Arthur's. Thor is a mighty warrior, a sky father. Shoshana was reluctant to give up that image and accept Arthur as a more real but less glamorous figure, as a father who could cry.

The child's movement towards individual identity must also become a movement away from family processes and family roles. To become a separate person, children must take on outside functions and learn to operate in the outside world with less and less help. As they grow, independence and self-reliance become more possible and more acceptable. First they become part of a more or less protective school environment. They begin to establish strong peer groups to achieve a sense of group identity outside the home. As they reach adolescence, outside-group identification may be stronger and more closely allied to the goals of the budding adult identity than participation in the family group. The family may feel like an obstacle rather than an aid in the path towards adult identity.

In most families, mother and home life are synonymous. In our culture, breaking away from the family is actually described as "cutting the apron strings." To the extent that the father is associated with the family's intimate processes as an earth parent, he too will be linked to the regressive emotions and old, childish patterns associated with home. However, the father is far more likely than the mother to be seen as a prominent symbol of the outside world. He is already out there, established in the very world that the child-turning-adult seeks to enter. In that world, he will be both a figure to be reacted against and a model to emulate, a force to run from and an ambition to be fulfilled. Most four-year-old boys proudly proclaim they want to be "just like Daddy." They see him in his powerful and admired position within the home. How many of these boys still say that they want to be like their fathers when they see them in relation to the outside world, when they are coming of age themselves?

Part of the mystique of the sky father is that the sons should grow up to be like their fathers no matter how little time the father actually spends with them. Such stories as that of King Arthur and the sword in the stone imply that there is a mystical bond through which the true successor will come into his own power. When young Arthur pulled the sword from the stone, it proved he was the rightful heir to the throne even though he himself did not know that he was the son of the dead king. Nothing that the earth parent can do will keep the son from his true calling—to be like his sky father.

The medieval hero Peredur (Percifal) was the son of a warrior-king who died in battle. His mother went to great trouble to raise Peredur in an atmosphere free from aggression. She would never allow any accouterments of war to come near him; he did not even learn the names of such objects. Yet when he came of age, he accidentally saw a knight on horseback in the forest. He was seized with an irresistible urge to become like that man. Inevitably, he went forth to become a warrior, revealing himself as his father's true son, even though he did not remember his father and had been raised exclusively by his mother.

Daughters, too, can feel compelled to grow up to be like their fathers, especially if they consider their mothers to be incompetent. One of the critical developmental factors in the psychology of successful professional women is a powerful positive identification with their sky father. Such women often literally follow in his footsteps, particularly if the society allows it. For example, it is interesting to note that Hugh Hefner's daughter has joined him as an executive of Playboy Enterprises. A generation ago, she would have been more likely to become a Playboy Bunny to get his attention than to join him as a colleague. The culture is supporting new avenues for women who want to gain intimacy with men, especially with men like their own sky fathers.

Myths like that of Peredur are very compelling, but real life does not always work out so smoothly. Peredur was able to romanticize a man he had never known. A real son—and daughter, too—gets to see the sky father at home, and the vision is not always appealing to the child.

Sometimes, the younger generation may decide that the father is an inadequate model to use as a bridge to the outside world. In upwardly mobile homes, or in first-generation immigrant homes, the parents may specifically teach the children to select other models. They want the children to do better or at least *other* than they themselves have done. Instead of being a direct model, such a parent can be a guide, pointing in the "right" direction and telling the child to get there on his own. But the child may be confused by the instructions to "do as I say, not as I do." It may be easier to react against everything the father stands for and to condemn him as a failure than to transcend the model he presents and find the positive image for which he stands. Many an adolescent son or daughter has confronted his or her father with the exasperated cry, "What do you *want* from me?"—a cry that arises out of the confusion between seeing the father as a model and hearing the father's further expectations, perhaps undefined but nevertheless present.

Even in homes that hope for continuity in generations, the child may become disenchanted with the father's values. He may then reject all parental advice and find another model, either from the dominant adult culture (probably as communicated through the media) or from the peer group. Thus the policeman's son becomes a delinquent, moving into open conflict with all men like his father, when he discovers his father is not as heroic as he had imagined—or, even worse, if he discovers real hypocrisy or corruption behind his father's expressed or assumed standards. So it is that the big businessman's son pleases his father by going to law school (getting the education his father never had time for) but uses it to become a labor lawyer, in open conflict with all his father stands for.

The distance and estrangement a son feels from his father can include the son's refusal to take the part the father has written for him. A short story written by a college student exposes this situation:

When Ben returned from Viet Nam, his father met him at the airport. He shook his hand and clasped his shoulder and told him physically that he loved him, that he was proud of him.

"By the way," his father told him in the car on their way home, "I told most of my friends that you were a captain in the Green Berets. If you happen to meet any of them would you not blow it for me? Would you tell them some bullshit about fighting, about leading?"

"Bullshit is right. Bullshit!"

The car was quiet, outside the night was quiet, and inside Ben there was noise.

"I can't do that! I'm not fucking good, but I'm not a fucking officer! I hate the army! I hate the war! I don't want to please you or your friends! You don't have to love me or be proud of me. I've done little to deserve either, but I'm not going to be your boy, adopt one, do something, but don't lay it on me."

There was nothing said anymore in that car and Ben was dropped off at his sister's apartment and there, alone, he laid down on her couch and slept without rest and dreamed of nothing.[1]

Once the sky father is no longer seen as god, all the smoldering negative feelings which have been subservient to the heroic imagery burst forth upon the now fallible man. When a son or daughter has torn down the paternal mask, his or her fear of the real man behind it may temporarily leave a feeling that there is no father, that he was always a fake, that even the good memories were unreal. Pity and disdain may become the dominant emotions of a child toward his or her father. Then the father himself may doubt his own growth as he feels his own powers waning as his children's strength grows. The child then looks down on the strange, weak father.

Contempt for and rejection of father can be accompanied by a deep fear. Thus Ed, a twenty-four-year-old computer salesman, developed acute anxiety about his success. He came for therapy. After a few weeks, he had a dream which clarified his inner turmoil:

I was in the house of my childhood. My father came up the porch stairs and knocked on the door. I was afraid to let him in because at his right hand was a ferocious lion. The lion seemed to be ignoring him. I was sure that I would be its target if it ever entered the house. I ran to my mother in the kitchen. She offered sympathy but gave

---

[1]From an unpublished story written by Kim Hoffman. Used by permission of the author.

little practical help. By this time the lion was inside. He stalked me from room to room with menacing growls. My father had disappeared; perhaps he had become the lion. I finally found a white powder in the cupboard. I fed it to the beast, hoping it was poison, but it didn't seem to work. I woke up, petrified, with the lion's breath still on my face.

Ed's father had been a failure in his work. He was genuinely proud of his son's success, but he was also very jealous of him. Ed felt his father's ambivalence but did not realize how great an impact it had on him. His mother, who had always protected him against his father when he was little, was useless in the outside world where the struggle was now taking place. The son tried to keep his father and the lion outside while he remained within, but it didn't work. The dream has no resolution; only the emotion of terror. Its message, however, was clear. Despite his age and achievement, Ed could not afford to see his father as a weak or irrelevant figure. His father still had power over him, at least in his unconscious mind. In the struggle between them, which had been going on since childhood, he could no longer rely on his mother as an ally. He was really on his own and was having difficulty facing the consequences of that.

In the act of rejecting the childhood image of father, some sons can get beyond fear and find transcendent emotions in approaching a new, unknown sense of self beyond the family's images. Such moments may signify the beginning of the young man's quest to find and shape his own future. Some children even refuse to acknowledge their real parents. Henrik Ibsen, James Joyce, D.H. Lawrence, Beethoven, and many other creative, intelligent, and sensitive men could not accept the inadequate men who were their fathers.

The fantasy of an alternate set of parents (and particularly of an alternate father) is common to many children who are unhappy with their families—and perhaps even to some who are not. They dream of being a prince or princess and hope their fantasy king or queen will rescue them from their ordinary surroundings. For many young people, it is galling to have an "ordinary" man as a past shadow inhibiting their most exhilarating hopes and dreams.

Perhaps the most dramatic examples of paternal rejection are found in religious young men who take on a "true" spiritual father to replace their earthly father. Almost all messianic figures do this. Jesus, son of a poor carpenter, decided at puberty that Joseph could not be his *true* father. He resolved this crisis in his own quest for a very special identity by dedicating himself to doing his "Father's work," that is, God's work. He lived out the fantasy of so many boys who are close to their mother and cannot accept their father as either a rival or a model by becoming the prophet of a religion in which his mother was a virgin and his father a divine and distant spirit, an ultimate sky father.

Fathers have a slightly different impact on daughters as they come of age. Traditionally, daughters have had a more limited struggle with their fathers; they do not have as many battlefields or as many lethal weapons for a confrontation. A daughter's choices are influenced by her father's approval and disapproval, fantasized or real. Her problem is discovering what will gain his approval. Girls often discover that they can please Daddy more by baking a cake than by succeeding on the baseball diamond, though some find that they can capture his attention most by being tomboys. Some daughters decide to be "just like Daddy" instead of competing with Mommy or other women.

Father and daughter may ally themselves against the wife-mother who, especially if she feels unsatisfied with the sky part of her own identity, will be more threatened than proud of an ambitious daughter.

A far more common element in the confrontation between father and adolescent daughter is the expression of sexuality. Fathers and daughters, even those who have cuddled and teased together within the family, are often unable to continue an affectionate relationship after the daughter reaches puberty. This is particularly true with sky fathers who have become romanticized in their role as outsiders. Suddenly a real liaison is possible. Many daughters use this as a weapon and express their rebellion by sexual acting out, by choosing a man (or men) their fathers don't approve of rather than choosing a career that would distress him.

The daughter's fantasy of gaining her father's attention is generally transferred to other men. For example, one young woman in therapy was irresistibly drawn to a career as a night-club entertainer. She would begin each performance by scanning the audience for a man who could be her father. She would find someone the right age and hold him in her gaze as she sang. She had never met her own father, although family legend had it that he frequented bars and entertainment spots. Another example is the anecdote—often paraded as a joke but almost certainly an actual event in more than one life—which tells of a young call girl who reported to a conventioneer's hotel room only to have the door opened by her own father, who was just as startled as she by the confrontation. The girl in this anecdote succeeded in discovering exactly what kind of women her father preferred!

Coming of age brings with it the need to establish an adult identity separate from that of the childhood family, a need to reevaluate the models of the past, especially the masculine model of the father, and make role and identity choices uniquely appropriate for the individual. This often entails re-bellion and rejection, sometimes simply in the service of es-cape, of breaking free, but often also out of a need to reject inappropriate or distasteful aspects of the parent.

It is often more comfortable to set up father as a hero or to be disillusioned and throw him off as a villain or an incompetent than to deal with the more complex reality of a man with human frailties and strengths. It may be particularly difficult to accept the waning power of the one man who has always been all-powerful and unchanging. Sooner or later virtually every child must confront the reality of surpassing his or her father, for the younger generation will still be in its prime when the older generation is in its decline. Thus it is almost inevitable that "coming of age" carries with it a component of "overthrow." There does not have to be any overt struggle. Most children do not actually kill their fathers. They just wait it out; time will make them, if not the winner, at least the survivor.

9

Reconciliation

When the child becomes a parent, the biological cycle of fathering is completed. Three generations face each other across time: grandfather, the original creator; parent, the new creator; and child, the potential creator. For the grandfather it is a crucial link in the chain of immortality; for the infant it is the infinite possibility of a beginning. For the new parent, still involved in the process of creating his or her own adult self, it is as much a new facet of self as the creation of a new life. All his or her relationships will change; marriage, interactions with parents, and, most of all, the sense of self as an individual. At first these changes will be gradual, almost imperceptible. They will deepen with time, outlasting other interests, transcending what seemed more immediate and relevant.

The traditional sky father may not have any concept that the act of having a child may profoundly change his life. One such man told us that he thought of his first baby as a "reward" for his wife who had worked for seven years while he went to graduate school. Now, at last, he had launched his career and was earning a lot of money, they could afford to live without her salary, and she deserved to have a child to be with while he was traveling. As he described it:

> It was central to her but not to me. I liked becoming a
> father the first time, but there was little special emotion
> attached to it. I remember thinking, "I'm a father who's
> going to be a scientist and explore the world." At best it

*added to my explorer identity. I felt two fantasies within
me: one for conquering the world, the other for family
life. The family fantasy meant little to me at the beginning.
It was my wife's thing. She did most of the raising.*

This man, John, was a true sky father. His research often
took him to wilderness areas for months at a time. He was
camping in the wastelands while his wife was pregnant, nursing, and diapering. He felt there was a rightness in the situation.
He was fulfilling his destiny as a sky father and had total trust
in the earth mother at home. He remembers sitting by the
campfire thinking, "Here I am conquering the world while my
wife is raising my family back at the hearth." It felt whole to
him.

Many men consider fathering as either irrelevant or even an
impediment to their growth and development as individuals.
Men who refuse to become fathers because of the toll it will
take on their personal aspirations are refreshingly honest. For
these men fathering *is* in competition with individual growth
and other forms of creativity. Many others acknowledge that
having children takes away time and competitive energy from
a successful career. Previously the "possession" of a family
was an advantage in business in the same way that a pretty
wife was good for the corporate image. But a man was certainly
not expected to devote much time to them.

In an agricultural community or in a family business, children rapidly became economic assets. They took over small
chores at an early age and eventually helped expand the economic base of the family. These reasons for having children
rarely apply any more. Children are enormously expensive.
No one now becomes a father with any illusion of financial
advantages.

Nevertheless, children do provide other comforts for their
parents. They stand against loneliness and provide companionship and meaning when the father's personal or work goals
seem unrewarding. They create a community, people to call,
to be with on holidays, to share joys and sorrows with. Unlike

friendships, parent-child relationships are likely to continue through good times and bad, through moves and fights and displacements and periods of dependence or resentment. There may be gaps that extend for years, but sooner or later a wedding or a funeral will bring the family together again. Then the father can identify with another life cycle than his own, watching the progress of his offspring from a safe distance.

A traditional sky father may have the greatest need for children because he is operating so completely in a reality devoid of nurturance. Like John, who needed to think of his wife at home with the children while he was out conquering the world, many sky fathers rely on their earth counterpart to fulfill the undeveloped aspect of themselves. They assume that there is no direct parental role to perform until the children are old enough to join them in the sky realm. Again, John states the position of the sky father:

Family and fathering were never critical determinants in my own personal transitions. I had to want to change. Then and only then could I test whether I would be valuable to them and they to me. It was never the other way around. My family's changes never directed my personal growth. But I was good at being a father of teenage daughters. They liked the kind of guidance and the model I provided. I was valueless before that time because I always wanted to foster their independence and they did not need that when they were little. They finally caught up with me, not me to them.

John's wife fulfilled the role of earth mother by supporting and shaping his relationship with his daughters. She was more protective and cautious than he, but she relied on him to lead the children out from her maternal influence. John found more and more things to do with his children as they grew older. By adolescence they were close companions.

In his individual search for meaning, a man like John must eventually discover a way to combine fathering with other male roles, especially to other forms of creativity. Fathering, no matter how it is carried forth from the moment of conception, is still the prototypic creative act for man. By becoming a father, he activates his potential to create and shape a new life. By becoming a father, he places himself beyond the pale of self-survival. Like all creative acts, but here more literally, he challenges his own mortality by creating something beyond himself. No matter how far a sky father may place himself from his family, he may grapple with the meaning of children and descendants to his own sense of a future that transcends his personal life.

Even as the father is assuring his immortality, he is threatening his own survival, for every father can feel the extent to which his children will need *his* creative energy as they grow, an energy in waning supply as he declines in his powers. This struggle for survival is as natural as the redwood sapling that will grow to tower over the parent tree and steal the sun from its leaves, or the young wolf who must eventually defeat his father in battle for pack leadership.

The story of Oedipus does not begin with the hero killing his father and marrying his mother—it begins with the father's attempt to kill his son. Laius, king of Thebes, is warned by an oracle that he would die at the hands of his son. For the ancient Greeks, the oracle was an outside voice of prophecy, although it is easier for most moderns to understand the oracle as something that resides within us, giving voice to our own unconscious hopes and fears.

The story of Oedipus tells us that the child is heir to the father's own fears of the son—even when that son's power is only potential, not actual. In the human situation, son killing is hidden behind initiation rites or nationalistic wars; fathers may claim that the gods demand blood sacrifice or that their political system is threatened, but it is always the sons who take the risk and spill the blood.

The father has to deal with his own urges to overwhelm or destroy his children; he also has to accept the inevitability that they will supersede him. Daughters are usually not threatening in the same direct way as sons, but they may promise danger also, the danger of being overwhelmed by an illicit sexual desire or, perhaps even more difficult, the almost inevitable danger of losing the beloved daughter to threatening younger men. Obsessive concern with how the girl dresses, strict rules about where she can go, whom she can see, and what hours she must keep, are all fears projected from the man's own impulses onto the world. He assumes that she will sexually arouse others and, perhaps, "get in trouble" because he experiences that response in himself. The father is thus in a very ambiguous relationship to other men who approach his daughter. On the one hand, he wants a man to make her happy and keep her safe and take the responsibility from him; on the other hand, he really wants to possess the girl himself, and so every young man who approaches her becomes a rival. Thus, forty-year-old fathers challenge their fourteen-year-old daughters' suitors to tennis matches, golf games, and motorcycle races in the hope of proving their masculine ascendancy but, very likely, pulling a muscle or otherwise humiliating themselves in the process.

Overidentification with a child is another form of mutual destruction. A child who lives his life for his parents' sakes has no idea of what it means to have a life of his or her own; a father who defers his personal aspirations for his child's sake is sacrificing a great deal of himself. Yet it is difficult, if not impossible, for a parent to take a child's successes and failures as events only in the child's life. A man is proud when his child is the star pitcher on the Little League team or the best student in the class. He is ashamed when his child is troublesome in school or unpopular among the children in the neighborhood. However he tries to distance himself from events, the behavior of the child seems to reflect on the self-image of the father. He may even be ashamed to find himself thinking smugly that he must be better than his best friend because his son received some distinction that his friend's did not.

A man who knew we were working on a book about fathering wrote us the following letter.

My experience in the past few weeks seems to me to be an example of the kind of drain that fathering can have on personal development—from a selfish point of view.

I have always been very successful professionally, as you know. I just took it for granted that my children would be part of my general success. I had kids like I had a career; they were both part of my bright-young-man image. I never really thought that the family would really affect my personal development or change the direction of my life. When you two spoke of fathering as having impact on adult development, that sounded like a novel idea, but I didn't really take it in. Now I realize how naive I have been.

Suddenly I find myself up against something in which I haven't been much of a success. It isn't me, exactly, and yet it is. It turns out that my son is dyslexic, and now they are also calling him hyperactive. I've always blamed people with those kinds of sons for not being good parents. What can I say now? Surely I've been as good a father as most. And Sally has been an excellent mother—or so I always thought. Now, of course, I'm not so sure. It's easiest to blame her. We are going through testing now. Perhaps it will all turn out to be the result of brain damage or an inherited defect. I'm not sure whether that would be good news or bad news. Are those things our fault? Could we have done something to avoid them?

The worst part has been watching him with his frustrations and failures in school. I've gotten mad and called him stubborn, and he has withdrawn more and more from the challenge. It has developed slowly. If it had been more dramatic, we would have caught on faster. But now that I am trying to face it squarely, I suddenly understand what fathers are doing when they leave their families. It was much nicer when I ignored the fact that he had a problem. I could go about my business and dream my dreams. When you are closely linked to people like this, they can drag you down. I thought children were supposed to cheer you up.[1]

This father is caught up in the midst of a fathering experience that he feels is inhibiting his development as an independent adult and is in no way enriching or ennobling him. Perhaps he is right. Perhaps there will be nothing in this crisis that will make him a better man. We suspect, however, that he will in fact gain both humility and compassion from this experience. His boy is not severely disturbed. His dyslexia will probably always be an annoying problem, but one that can be worked with. The feelings that the father took for granted in himself have been shaken. Now they will be based on something more substantial than pride.

Most bonds are best recognized when tested; the fathering bond is extreme in this regard. Over and over again in our interviews and in psychotherapeutic work with men, we have found that the recognition of the true strength of the fathering identity was only apparent in moments of crisis. Men who do not consciously acknowledge the depth of their feelings for their children find themselves overwhelmed when they must face separation from them.

Many fathers experience difficulties when their families break apart. Men who have ostensibly devoted themselves to public life, to the pursuit of power, money, and prestige, suddenly find their achievements hollow in the face of a lost or alienated child. Career efforts may symbolically stand as a legacy for their children. A man may suddenly realize for the first time that what he thought of as personal motivation really drew its energy from his relationships with his children and with his own father. Achievements take on special meanings when a man is a father himself.

One of the great paradoxes in the psychology of the mature father is that involvement with his own parents, especially his father, increases with his own parenthood. Perhaps it is the beginning confrontation and potential outdistancing by his own

---

[1] Used by permission.

child that rekindles a need for identification and reconciliation with the older generation. Arthur had a dream that spoke clearly to this feeling:

> *I am running up a long hill and Jonah, my oldest boy, is in front of me. I am aware that I am probably a faster runner, but he still is outdistancing me. He is wearing my good blue Adidas running shoes, while I have on the black shoes I wear while doing psychotherapy. Mine keep falling off and slowing me down. But I notice that he runs very fast and well. I think that I should ask him his secret and tell him some secrets of mine. I wake up thinking that I must tell my father how much he helped me learn to be a man.*

Fathers learn from becoming and being fathers. Part of that learning may come directly from the child itself, not only from the feelings, memories, responsibilities, and events that are part of fathering, but also from the unique encounter between parent and child. Children are remarkable teachers. Some say that the child is father to the man. This means that the small child within us effects our development—but it may also mean that a child may teach his own father in a different way than any other teacher because there is so much of the father inside him. Children take on the unconscious characteristics of their parents, act out their vicarious wishes, play the scenarios that the parents were unable to carry out themselves. No matter how hard they try to let them be themselves, parents project their own wishes onto their children. As the child matures, parents can recognize unused parts of themselves in them. Perhaps that is why it is so hard to talk to children, particularly adolescents and young adults who are "know-it-alls." They know what is most threatening to their parents. They know and experience what the parents did not want to know and experience. But wise parents can transcend the resistance to hearing the darker, more unknown parts of themselves that are brought to daylight by their children.

It is difficult for a person to truly encounter his or her own children; it may be even harder to truly encounter his or her own father. One of the most intriguing findings in recent studies of middle-aged men is the role of an older mentor or guide in their lives even when they seem to have reached a stage of independence and success.[2] Men still seem to need a wise old man to support them, especially if they are becoming teachers and guides in their own right. Perhaps it is easier for a mature person to make another man over into a father figure than to come to terms with his own father. The feelings with a mentor are more diluted; the relationship can remain idealized. A face-to-face reconciliation with one's own father brings out the unacceptable regressive tendencies, the memories of being a child under his thumb or of the senseless rebellion against his authority in adolescence. Many fathers and their mature sons make the mistake of assuming that their relationship can become like any two adults, based on liking or not liking each other as persons. This is difficult, if not impossible, to achieve. Father is always laden with the aura of the role. The image may be replaced by some other parent, a god, or a teacher, someone who is easier to see than the flesh and blood parent. The mentor may play this role.

As we write this book, we are both at that time in our personal life cycles when reconciliation with our parents is more possible than ever before. We are both more secure in our marriage and our careers than we were when we were younger. More important, we have been parents long enough to realize the difficulties and the limitations of our position. We can empathize more closely with the feelings our own parents must have had as they guided our development. We have reached the age that our parents were when we were in school—we even look like the parents we remember from our own childhoods.

Libby's parents are both dead now. Although she was on

[2] The role of the mentor has been stressed by Daniel Levinson and his co-workers in their study of American men during their mid-adult years. (See Daniel Levinson and others, *Seasons of a Man's Life*. New York: Ballantine, 1978.)

very good terms with them in their last years, she finds that there is still work to be done:

I find that I am still reevaluating my relationship with my parents and still think of them often. At first it was very difficult; I felt great remorse and guilt for all the things that hadn't gone perfectly between us. I was obsessed with conversations that should have taken place and never did and with conversations that did take place and never should have. I felt liberated from the burden of their expectations and felt guilty about that. I felt despair at their absence when I needed a confidant, especially when I needed help about issues in my marriage or with my children. But gradually (and the process has been going on now for six years) I started to let go of the remorse, stopped being angry at the injustice of it all. This transformation has taken place largely through dream encounters. At first it was frightening and horrible to have them come to me in my dreams. They were dead, and they came laden with the aura of death. Then I started to have different kinds of dreams in which they were alive and well, although old and slowed down as they had been in their last years. But one morning I woke up feeling unusually refreshed. My father had come to me as a young man, even younger than I could remember him from my childhood. He was slim and dark-haired, strong and slightly ironical. We picked apples together and talked about how my career was going and whether I was happy with my life. The conversation was very like many I had had with him when I was making college and career choices in young adulthood and he was approaching retirement in his mid-sixties. But in my dreams we could transcend time and be of the same age simultaneously.

Both of Arthur's parents are alive, and there has been more time for the growth of a different relationship between them. He describes two kinds of meetings, one in the form of a dream,

the other in a particularly meaningful encounter, which have
contributed to his reconciliation:

*Several years ago I had a dream during a particularly
happy time of my life. My youngest son, Ari, had been
born two years before. I had come from a family of only
two children, and my third still felt a little out of focus.
For some weeks before the dream, I was aware how important Ari had become to me. I was filled with more and
more joy with my family. I also recognized that some of
those feelings came from a childish sense of having bested
my father by having more children than he. It was a
ludicrous emotion to feel, but it kept coming up in my
fantasies. That was my internal state when I had my
dream.*

*I was by the ocean, feeling particularly strong and virile.
I was unashamedly reveling in the water, watching the
waves pour across my body and run through my beard,
when suddenly I was transformed into Poseidon. He had
always been a favorite god of mine; now I was Poseidon
completely, and the vitality I had been experiencing mul-
tiplied enormously. Then, without warning, I began to
cry. Suddenly I felt myself breaking an eggshell which
had been encasing me. I emerged from the fragmented,
gelatinous shell with an acute awareness that I was A
Father. I knew that the shell of the egg was the skin of
my own father and that by bursting it I had killed him. I
had burst out of his skin, breaking him apart. His destruction was my birth as a mature father. I continued to
cry and to laugh as the meaning of all this flooded through
me. In the dream it was very real—his death and my
birth. When I woke up and pondered its meaning, I saw
it more as destroying that part of him that remained as a
restraint inside of me.*

*In this dream I broke through the barriers of my sonhood
and destroyed my father's hold on me. I felt that I had*

*destroyed the image that he had set for me and had gone
beyond anything he could imagine to create my own definition of what a man (and a father) could be.*

*When I look at my own sons, I see how much they admire
me now. But they also feel anger toward me. They want
to learn what I can teach, but they want to go beyond me
as well. One of them talked about what would happen
someday "when I grow up and you grow down." That
expresses the feeling. It is as if the seed of my destruction
walks beside me.*

*For a time after the dream, it was very hard to be with
my own father in real life. I felt an irrational guilt about
what I had done to him. Gradually it became easier, and
our relationship changed for the better. I felt much more
separate from him and could see him more clearly as a
person. The father-son relationship continued, though its
actual influence over me was lessened.*

*Two years later I had an experience with him that changed
our relationship even more. My father is above all a man
of reason, of plans, and of strategies. It is more than his
training in the law; it is a basic personality structure. He
disapproved of my taking art and music in college because
there was no telling how badly I might do. I might jeopardize my future along with my grade point average. When
I got A's in these subjects he was relieved, but hoped that
I would "settle down" and stop taking risks. In the same
way, my training in psychiatry seemed senseless to him.
Why had I learned so many medical skills to throw them
away? Similarly, turning away from academic life towards
"uncharted" areas in writing and therapy seemed unwise.
What assurance had I that books would sell? How did I
know that patients would come? Why wasn't I planning
for the future? We argued incessantly. Eventually he
turned his advisory talents to my brother's career. He is
a scientist and Dad finds his choices more understandable.*

Strangely, when I went into a Jungian analysis and then joined the Jungian Institute, his interest in my career revived. He said he could understand my need to join an institute and gain the additional prestige and referral sources that it would provide. He saw it as an overdue step towards securing myself as an established psychiatrist. But why not the Freudian Institute? Weren't they better known and more respected? Wouldn't I lose out because of the occultish tinge to Jung's work? Of course he understood that I wouldn't associate myself with charlatans, but would everyone understand the reasons for my choice?

Try as I would, I didn't seem to be able to talk with him about my personal reasons for wanting Jungian training. Instead, I entered into the old arguments. I emphasized the practical realities in San Francisco, the history of the two institutes there, the local politics, the probable future trends in psychiatry. Once again we were in conflict around career strategies. Once again I felt alienated from my father as I'm sure he did from me.

This time I pondered more closely what had gone wrong. The issue was no longer "success," at least not at the rational level. He was doing particularly well as a lawyer, involved in exactly the kind of practice he had always hoped for. I was increasingly well known, my books were published and widely read, I had more than enough psychotherapy work, I was financially secure. Why then had I taken up his challenge at the level of career plans rather than talking about the inner changes that my decision to study Jungian psychology reflected? I remembered that, when I had tentatively talked to him about dream analysis, meditation, and my own spiritual quest, he had commented that he tried to forget his dreams because they were unpleasant and then changed the subject. Clearly my interests were threatening to him. I had assumed that he couldn't or wouldn't understand and secretly con-

gratulated myself on charting a path that he couldn't follow. For me, at least, the issues seemed the same as feelings of childish pride at having one more child than he.

On the other hand, I remembered that I had talked easily with my mother about my shifting interests. We both agreed that Dad wouldn't understand because his inner life was unfamiliar and scary to him. It was easy to see through that pattern. I was still in rebellion, still fighting a family battle for my mother. Perhaps I was selling him short, unwilling to risk facing him with my own strengths and sharing them with him. So I stopped talking about the future with him and started talking on the subjective present and my inner life. At first it was extremely difficult, but soon it became more and more intriguing. One day I asked him directly for a gift. I asked him for a shofar, a ritual ram's horn. He didn't take my request seriously. In truth, the voice asking for it was very weak. But gradually, as I repeated my interest, I detected more interest from him. I told my father of a dream I had had in which my spirit had pierced an ominous grey cloud which blocked praying souls from reaching heaven. I mentioned a story I had read as a child of the power of a shrill child's cry in carrying an oppressed people's message to God. I wondered if a shofar would help me in my meditations.

I felt crazy talking about such things with my father—a man of reason, grandson of an anti-Hassidic rabbi, a man who eschewed mysticism as well as his own dreams. But months later, he told me in a trembling voice that he had located a shofar for me. It took many months to deliver it to my hands, for we were both aware of the change it signified in our relationship. With his gift, the most meaningful I have ever received, was a letter which I quote in part:

"In the past 47 years I have frequently given gifts. I have given them with love, with affection, with satisfaction, with thanks. Never have I experienced that indescribable thrill associated with your shofar. The suggestion from you; the search; the communications; the unexpected guide; the finding; the verification. The first blast in my own office when my associates came in thinking that I had either pushed the calendar back or forward to Rosh Hashana. Then bringing it home and wrapping it tenderly and carefully before delivery to you. . . . A long blast from a ram's horn leveled the walls of Jericho. Your interest is not earthbound. Your shofar is destined not only to break barriers, but to break through barriers to Jerusalem and beyond for higher fulfillment. May it be so."

The letter speaks for itself. For me, it is his blessing of the direction which I have chosen for my life. For him, it is a glimpse of his son's purpose. Perhaps, too, it is an understanding of something hidden in himself. If so, my gift to him is at least the equal of his to me.

The process of reconciliation with the father is never-ending and continues through death and beyond. To come to terms with a personal creator, a passionate love object, an image of power and destruction; to love and hate the man himself as well as the man within the paradoxical and transcendent role of father is a supreme integration, one which is difficult to manage, except in the context of a religious or mystical experience. Some of the older people we talked with in our interviews, particularly those whose fathers had died, were able to hint of such an element in their experience of being fathered. One expressed it as a kind of telepathy between himself and his deceased father, a man he had struggled against and hated all his life.

It began when I went out to my trailer, parked by the ocean, to escape a particularly vicious battle between my son and my wife. I felt the need to talk to someone, but there was no one there to help. On a whim, I picked up the disconnected radio phone, lying unused on the shelf, and listened to a grainy noise inside, like listening to a seashell. Suddenly I heard the voice of my father, first faintly and then as clear as if he were right there. The voice was talking about the problems he used to have with his son, me. Nothing more profound, just everyday problems. And then it all became clear. The mystery of fathering, the inevitability of conflict, the disillusion. The pettiness of hoped-for thanks from your kids. And the pervasive sense of a kind of cosmic love that went with seeing and understanding the cycle.

Reconciliation of this kind may not be possible before middle age. It requires the humility of maturity and a recognition that the child has not been infallible as a person or as a parent any more than the father had been. It is an acceptance of father and, as deeply, an acceptance of self and of life as something that must be struggled with but not necessarily conquered.

This chapter has taken the child's experience of one kind of father, the sky father, from earliest consciousness to middle age, to the point at which the child achieves genuine empathy and acceptance of the father's personhood—in fact, to the point at which the child is as old as his father had been. This is the point we have reached in our own lives. We know that *father* will continue to be an important theme in our lives, but, increasingly, the meaning of that theme will be related to our own choices and the projections we receive from our descendants. We are the parental generation. By the time we become grandparents, the struggle with the preceding fathers will be a memory, an abstraction. The word "father" will call to mind "children" more rapidly than the image of "Dad."

It is hard to give up the hope of father, the wish for him to be there, either as a real person or as a protective spirit. When father's power is waning, children feel betrayed, abandoned, and alone. Death of father can be an absolute confrontation with helplessness, frailty, and the implacable, unyielding movement of time and fate across a life that had contained some illusion of safety. To the extent that father represents security and authority, the loss of father brings insecurity and chaos. Governments know this well and institute careful rules to follow in the frightening hours that follow the demise of a ruler.

"The king is dead! Long live the king!" Within this paradox hides a necessary truth. A new father emerges even before the old one is gone. The younger generation becomes old and in the process assumes the mantle of power—a mantle no longer romantic or glittering but weighty and burdensome. It takes a brave man to say "the buck stops here." It is far easier to pass the buck on to *him*, on to the "real" father. It may be even easier to blame him for not doing a better job. "If he'd been more understanding/around more/more competent, then I'd be able to do a better job . . . "

Reconciliation means getting beyond fear, getting beyond anger, getting beyond rejection, and accepting the role of father not in its optimistic aspects as creator and up-and-coming power but in its full weight of being the generation of authority, the one who must do the protecting, the providing, and the caring for all other generations, younger and older.

The oldest person we interviewed was an eighty-six-year-old great-grandfather. He had already been retired for twenty years. Although his job was important to him, and his hobbies still kept him busy, it was his awareness of himself as a father that seemed most central to his life. He recalled his own father in clear detail. He was also full of images from his own career as a young father—a time when he tried very consciously to do better than his rather cold, aloof parent had done. He knew the exact date of every marriage, birth, and divorce in his family. He could tell us exactly how old each of his descendants was at any moment. He felt that one of his most important roles had been to act as a refuge for his grandchildren as they struggled with their parents in adolescence and as young adults. He was far more critical of his children than of his grandchildren. He was never surprised to find a distressed twenty-year-old on his doorstep. A granddaughter came to him for help during an illegitimate pregnancy; a grandson came to confess his confusion over drugs and sex. He babysat for great-grandchildren and acted as go-between from one generation to the other. He was past the struggle for dominance or for success, beyond earth and sky modes of parenting. He displayed with equal pride the orange tree planted by his grandson, the gardener, and the book published by his grandson, the professor. He recognized the patterns that he lived through in his time when he saw them in the younger generation. His experience as a father had its ups and downs, but it led inevitably to his experience as a grandfather, which enriched and enlightened his old age. He was beyond reconciliation and beyond power struggles, but not beyond fathering.

It is difficult for a man to accept gracefully the waning of his power. If he had invested energy in fathering, he may experience his own loss of strength as a proud but retired leader who has guided his younger generation to successful fruition. If he has had failures, or if fate destroyed his children and left him alone, he may be either bitter or desperately lonely. Much of fathering is up to chance. There is no absolute correlation between "good" fathering and "good" children. There are far too many factors at work. Much that a man does in his role as father is determined by patterns that lie deep within him, established in his own childhood and lodged in his unconscious, not easy to recognize and even more difficult to alter. Nevertheless, each man can work to make some conscious choices. He can conceptualize what he wants for himself and his family and attempt to transform the raw material of fatherhood into a viable style for his family.

As he moves through his adult life, a father must continue to engage in the process of evaluating his personal development. Part of the process is to understand the role and meaning of father and fathering to him as he continues to evolve as a person and as a member of the family group.

PART III

The Nontraditional Father

This last section of the book will deal with the problems and possibilities for men who want to follow a nontraditional path in fathering. In Chapter 10 we will address the question of whether or not men are actually capable of being earth parents and present experimental and life history evidence which suggests that they are indeed well equipped to raise their children—if they choose to do so. In Chapter 11 we will investigate what happens when a man decides that he *does* want to be intimately involved with each stage of parenting: How can he express his identity as a father, especially during the first year when the mother's part seems so much more important? How will a committed earth father feel about his all-too-obvious limitations during pregnancy, birth, and nursing? How will he transcend these limits in order to establish a meaningful relationship with the fetus and the infant?

In Chapter 12 we will describe the various ways men have struggled to free themselves from the sky father heritage and have incorporated other images of fathering. We will look particularly closely at men who have established themselves as either earth fathers or dyadic fathers and see how they kept alive their sense of connectedness to their children after their initial experience as creator and as early nurturer. We will consider their conflicts and problems as well as their joys and

successes. We will also look at the surprise with which some
traditional men discover their own potential in the earth realm
after they have become established fathers.

In Chapter 13 we will speculate on the implications that
nontraditional fathering may have for the children. How will
an earth father affect his children? How do children develop
when they are faced with a father who contradicts major cultural
assumptions? What are the advantages and disadvantages for
children with parents who are less traditional?

We hope that Part Three will help the unconventional minority of families who embrace nontraditional patterns towards
a sense of clarity and confidence in their parenting and help
the traditional majority realize their style as a conscious and
appropriate choice rather than an inevitable burden.

10

Men As Earth Parents

In recent years, more and more men have been questioning their sky roles. Some young men are beginning to reject the models of fathering provided by their own sky fathers and are searching for new ways to become men and to parent.[1] Some older men, disillusioned with the competitive and aggressive sky world, are turning toward more gentle pursuits. A radical restructuring of maleness and fatherhood is under way. The earth father image is exploding into consciousness, demanding exploration and recognition.

Among the four archetypes we have traced, the sky father image alone is devoid of the nurturant aspects of parenting. The other three require male involvement in domestic details. The earth father requires a sky mother as a complementary opposite, for the father does not function in the sky realm.

---

[1] One study of families of corporate executives revealed that only nine out of seventy children between the ages of seventeen and twenty-four were planning to go into corporate careers like their fathers. (See Patricia Brooks, "Whatever Happened to 'Following in Dad's Footsteps'?" TWA *Ambassador*, May 1977, pp. 18–20.) The overwhelming majority of subjects in this study said that they were going to enter service jobs such as medicine, psychology, and special education. They talked about intangible rewards and human values and of having a life in which they would not have to move a lot. They said that they did not want to be like their sky fathers, who were never around the house. The men in this group have chosen to devote themselves to nurturant roles, though still focused in the work setting. They did value children and home in a way that might lead them to earth fathering, even though they lacked models for it in their own childhoods.

Both royal and dyadic fathers combine earth and sky realms within themselves, the royal father by taking both into himself and excluding the female, the diadic father by sharing earth and sky functions in syzygy with a female partner.

Our personal hope for the future of parenting is in the dyadic image. This is our own style, but we also feel that it provides the most practical and humanistic way for both parents to get what they want from their work and their family. Many women want to partake of the sky realm without sacrificing their roles in the earth realm altogether; simultaneously, many men want to explore their own nurturance capabilities in the family. The dyadic mode allows for both, if father and mother are willing to give up some traditional prerogatives in exchange for what they gain.

Most men still work in the sky world and model their parenting style on the sky father. In the hope of discovering other fathering potentials, we sought out men who seemed to be unusually nurturant and involved in family life when we interviewed for this book. To our surprise, we found that most of them were disillusioned and filled with conflict as they looked back on their careers as fathers. They cared a lot about family life, but most of them were still fundamentally sky fathers. Their disappointment came in part from the fact that they didn't really think of their sky role as *parental*. They thought of their careers and the need to make a living as being in conflict with family life. It did not occur to them that their outside activities *were* the fathering that they were doing. They cherished the moments of intimacy with their children, yet felt guilty that they were not more available more often. Faced with their own parenting as an object of study, these sky fathers experienced the same bittersweet feeling that children of sky fathers describe. They felt it was a shame that practical financial and career issues had interfered with family life. With few exceptions, these fathers said they were unhappy that outside attachments had limited their relationships with their children.

Our interviews probably provoked a guilty reaction and made men think they should emphasize their nurturant component. Most were defensive about the topic, as if they had somehow failed to do a job they had never really defined. Many commented that, in other settings, particularly in male groups (at work or in leisure time), the subject of fathering rarely came up. One man admitted that, in five years of psychoanalysis, he had rarely discussed his feelings about being a father.

In other words, the men we chose to interview because of their involvement in their families all felt that they somehow fell short of their ideal parenting goals. They felt that they had been forced by circumstances to take a role that was more aloof from the family than they had wished. Most of these men also felt that they had had a concept of perfect fathering, but that somehow they had never been able to actualize it.

Most of these men felt that they had experienced enormous early fathering potential that somehow was lost along the way. A father we will call Roy told us his experience:

One day, soon after my first child was born, I was sitting in my den in my old rocker. I was holding my son in my arms. Suddenly I sensed that I would do anything for him, that I would lay down my life for him. The feeling focused in a single vision. If the lion was coming, I'd stand between him and the wild beast.

The strange thing was that it never happened again that way. I never felt it again, that kind of flow. It was very powerful, but it faded and never returned. Fathering for me was always difficult, not ecstatic. I labored through it, filling the role with failed purposes. And yet I still remember that vision as the real meaning, the first and only time I understood.

If the lion was coming, I'd stand between him and the wild beast.

This vision is prototypic of the sky father as protector and guardian of the household, yet it also contains a universe of nurturance and caring ready to be developed. Unfortunately, Roy lived in a suburban parsonage rather than a village hut.

There were no lions to fight off; the only "wolf at the door" would be hunger if he didn't earn a large enough pay check to buy groceries. The struggle for survival was hardly mythic or ennobling for Roy as a father. He felt that his vision could have become central to his experience of fatherhood, but that it did not.

Roy did not believe that he should function as a direct nurturer to his children. He felt he would lose his individuality and his masculinity if he tried to care for his family. He was both unprepared and unwilling to venture into the earth world of mothers.

Roy firmly believes that, as a function of their anatomy, women have special skills and intuitions about child care which men cannot duplicate. At the heart of Roy's choice to become a sky parent and focus his nurturance in the community rather than in his family was a firm belief that he would be unable to compete with his wife in the earth realms, just as she would be unable to compete in the sky realms.

Sex-role stereotyping along earth and sky lines is sometimes so artificial that it becomes ludicrous. We have seen wise and gentle male pediatricians, capable of the most complex and loving behavior toward their infant patients, defer to their painfully inexperienced wives as to the best way to diaper a newborn or calm a distressed three-month-old. In the early years of our own family, Arthur, who had had months of experience with babies in emergency wards and clinics, would often watch from a distance as Libby fretted and fumbled with a sick child. Less dramatically, we have observed warm, nurturant men give up all the parenting of their children to cold, aloof wives who had little interest in or talent for the job. These are examples where stereotypes and conditioning have gotten in the way of rational decision making about who is more competent to perform one or another parenting function.

We do not dismiss sex-role stereotypes in parenting altogether. Pregnancy and the capacity to breast-feed are important physical and psychological factors. Nevertheless, we feel that men's capacity to nurture should be examined more closely. How much parenting is part of a male's biological heritage?

How much can he learn to overcome any inborn discrepancies between himself and his wife?

We cannot generalize directly from animal studies, but some findings from laboratory and field observations are suggestive of the human situation and may help clarify the potential of the adult male to take on earth functions. Among primates, it seems to be true that the mother is almost always the primary caretaker. Monkey mothers spontaneously care for their infants immediately after birth. However, this is not an absolute phenomenon. In the laboratory, Harry Harlow produced female monkeys who did not perform normal earth functions.[2] They were female rhesus monkeys who had been removed from their own mothers at birth and reared in isolation. When these monkeys were impregnated and gave birth, they failed to perform normal maternal functions for their infants. In the wild, Goodall has documented a chimpanzee mother who became an infant killer and taught her children to help her kidnap, kill, and eat the infants of other mothers.[3]

If female monkeys can sometimes be incompetent at earth functions, can male monkeys sometimes be good at them? The answer seems to be yes.[4] In at least one primate species, the father seems to be the more nurturant and protective parent. The infants go to the mothers to nurse but cling to the fathers most of the time. While this does not occur as a general rule in other species, observers in the field have occasionally reported incidents in which male monkeys have assumed full responsibility for the care of young. This seems to happen under special circumstances. Generally, male monkeys give no evidence of distinguishing between their own offspring and other babies in the troop; however, they are more likely to be protective of infants belonging to a female to whom they are

[2]H. F. and M. K. Harlow, "Learning to Love," *American Scientist* 54 (1966):244–72.
[3]Jane Goodall, "Life and Death at Gombe," *National Geographic* 115 (May 1979): 592–621.
[4]William K. Redican, "Adult Male-Infant Interactions in Nonhuman Primates," *The Role of the Father in Child Development*, Michael E. Lamb, ed. New York: John Wiley, 1976, pp. 345–85.

attached. Thus they may care for their own mother's younger offspring but chase away other infants; they also tend to be more nurturant toward the offspring of their own mate than others. Field observers have recorded a male member of the troop taking on the full care of a motherless infant old enough to survive without breast milk but not yet old enough to take care of itself. This suggests that the male may stand second in line and take over only when something goes wrong with the mother. Laboratory studies confirm that "stepfather" monkeys were willing and able to take over as parent and showed grief when their adopted baby was removed from their care.

If an adult rhesus monkey can learn to care for a baby, surely human males can do the same. In fact, there are a few human

Figure 22. Barbary Macaque Male and Infant. Males in some primate species are nurturant and protective of the young. This Barbary macaque male (father?) has assumed the position characteristic of macaque mothers as he shelters this infant. (Photograph courtesy of David Taub, Ph.D., Yemassee Primate Center, Yemassee, South Carolina.)

cultures in which the male does far more than step in if the mother is missing or incompetent.

Among the Manus of New Guinea (when Margaret Mead studied them),[5] the men went fishing before dawn; they returned early, drowsy from hours of work and content to play with the children all day while the women worked. They started caring for a baby as soon as possible, at first cuddling it, tickling it, blowing on its arms, and otherwise playing with it. They left the harsh training to the mother. When she had taught it to cling around the neck and not to fall in the water or touch the fire, he would take the child out in his boat and paddle to grand adventures on islands where women were forbidden. Not surprisingly, children experienced their fathers as attentive and joyous, their mothers as harsh and dull. Mead describes the family interaction:

> *It is a frequent picture to see a little minx of three leave her father's arms, quench her thirst at her mother's breast, and then swagger back to her father's arms, grinning overbearingly at her mother.*[6]

The mother was often abused by the husband and his relatives in front of her children. The boys and girls inherited the spirits of their father's household; they grew up in the atmosphere of his people. Inevitably, they developed allegiance to their father, their siblings, and their own village, not to their mother, who was little more than a useful object for them. But it is particularly revealing to note that when Mead introduced dolls to the tribe, it was the *boys* who spontaneously played with them. In this culture where the earth parent was male, it was the males who wanted to play with and care for what we would call "girlish" toys.

Support for potential of an earth role for fathers is beginning

[5]Margaret Mead, *Growing Up in New Guinea,* from *The South Seas: Studies of Adolescence and Sex in Three Primitive Societies,* Vol. 2. New York: Morrow, 1939, p. 73. Copyright 1930, 1958, 1962 by Margaret Mead.
[6]Ibid., p. 168.

to come from behavioral scientists who study family interactions. The fact that predominately male researchers are even considering paternal behavior as relevant to child development is itself an indication of a significant change in the legitimacy of the father's role within the family. Entire theories have given the father no role whatsoever during the first three years of life. Psychotherapists rarely deal with the father in their treatment of children's difficulties.

Much of the recent work on fathering suggests that there is a distinct minority of men who are involved as earth fathers even in the earliest phases of their children's development. For example, Pederson and Robson found that six out of the forty-five fathers in their study engaged in intimate caretaking activities, with an average of eight hours per week in play activity. Three fourths of the children in their study showed intense attachment to their fathers.[7]

Ernst Abelin's study of very early fathering among eleven men also identified a small group of fathers who demonstrated strong nurturance.[8] His research, part of an ongoing project whose purpose was an intense description of the early mother-child pair, found that a "stranger reaction" toward the father was unusual. Five of the eleven children were said to *prefer* their fathers to their mothers by the time they were nine months old. For example, Abelin described a boy of six months who reacted more positively to his father's voice than to his mother's and who relaxed better in his father's arms. He also described a little girl who preferred her father until she was 20 months old. Abelin explains both these cases in terms of an inadequacy in the mother-child relationship, an inability of the child to establish early basic trust. Because of this deficiency, the father's emotional involvement was seen as critical to the child's capacity for object relations. This analysis of the situation assumes that something must be wrong with the mother before

---

[7] F. A. Pederson and K. S. Robson, "Father Participation in Infancy," *American Journal of Orthopsychiatry* 39 (1969):466–72.

[8] Ernest L. Abelin, "The Role of the Father in the Separation-Individuation Process," *Separation-Individuation*, J. B. McDevitt and C. F. Settlage, eds. New York: International Universities Press, 1971. pp. 229–52.

the father will play such an important role in the child's development. The investigators do not suggest the possibility of a father who is simply better skilled in empathy and "mutual cueing" than his wife, though we feel certain that such husband-wife pairs do exist; we have observed them informally ourselves.

All these studies strongly suggest that men and women have accepted the aphorism that "biology is destiny" too literally. The advantages a woman may gain from her specialized reproductive system do not necessarily limit a man's nurturant and relational abilities any more than a man's larger size and musculature limit a female's potential assertiveness in the sky world.

If a man in our society wants to explore the possibility of being an earth father, he should realize that the role has more to do with personal choice than with instincts. Men do not lack the ability to be earth parents. The real issues are, first, choosing the image for oneself; second, accepting what must be given up as well as what may be gained; and third, establishing a relationship with a partner who will support the choice.

Changes in the male image towards the incorporation of more nurturance and less "machismo" are slowly taking place among child-free young adults. Most men do not think about how all this will affect the choice of a fathering role until pregnancy begins. Every once in a while, however, we meet a man who is conscious of the issues even before fatherhood is imminent in his own life.

Alan was such a man. For him, marriage was a choice that hinged on whether or not to become a father. He found a woman he enjoyed and loved, but he could not make a strong commitment to her until he resolved the issue of becoming a father. He entered therapy and soon realized that much of the problem lay in his rejection of his own father, whom he saw as a plastic sky father and as a failure. He began to dream of his long-dead paternal grandfather, a man he had almost forgotten. This grandfather had lived in the coastal mountains in California on a small piece of wooded property. In Alan's memory, he was entirely taken up with the land. He raised fruit trees, vegetables, and herbs. In Alan's mind he was a modern "ancestor king" who drew his creative energies from the earth. In his dreams, Alan went to him and always felt renewed and invigorated when he woke up. He saw this man as an inner ally who gave him depth. He saw his own father as superficial, the product of business success and tarnished by excessive ambition and competitiveness.

There is something very meaningful in a young man's inner search for a *fathering* image in a grandfather who is wholly occupied in tending the land. Alan was looking for the intimate nurturant potential that could be more immediate than the role of economic provider. It may be that when he has children, Alan will find himself absorbed in sky functions and have little need to be linked with the earth. At the time of this writing he has married and is contemplating a child. He has a clearer image of earth father than before; he hopes to use it as a model for his own parenting.

Alan's aggrandizement of the land and his desire to be a different kind of parent than his own father is a familiar refrain among men today. The image of earth father has great appeal, not only as a parenting style but as a way of life. In fact, an earth father will call on the softer, more nurturant and receptive aspects of his personality in order to be creative in the role. At the same time, he will also limit the more aggressive and striving parts of his personality. For most men, such a shift is tantamount to a reorientation away from traditional masculine values and traditional masculine behaviors. Being an earth father is not a matter of being warm and intimate with a child at home and then becoming competitive and hard driving at work. The difference between the earth and sky modes may be too basic to allow rapid transitions on a day-to-day basis. Men (or women) cannot come home from a high pressure day at the office and magically turn into receptive and gentle parents as soon as they walk in the door. Sooner or later, one mode will predominate, and that will usually be the conventional one. We know men who feel they need to smoke marijuana in order to enjoy caring for their child. Without it they are impatient and nervous with the little details that are the essence of earth parenting. Alcohol is also used by many to help make the transition across the boundary between the outside world and the family.

People who become fully committed earth parents often discover that the aggressiveness with which they pursue their careers diminishes as they adjust to the needs of children and that the outside job becomes flat and meaningless compared to the importance of the family. This may be frightening to men who seek an image of themselves as involved fathers but who do not really want to be changed in the process. We feel that it is virtually inevitable that a man's inner and outer life will change as a result of a deepening investment in the intimate process of parenting. Unions, corporations, and professional organizations know this well. They may give lip service to their junior executives' maintaining family involvement, but usually they mean just keeping up an outward show of traditional patriarchal virtues. It is tacitly understood by those in power that at some point a choice must be made between family and career if a man is to "get ahead." Like a woman who assumes that her career will take second place to her involvement as a mother, an earth father sees his fathering as coming first. He often changes his work to find something that is more consonant with his parental functions. Professionals may become writers, academics and businessmen may run workshops and classes out of their homes to be able to spend more time with the kids and have more freedom and control over their working hours. Continuous institutional commitments require meetings and administrative work that cut into family hours. For an earth father, the family is the primary, if not the only, institution.

Most men are unwilling and unable to make a major change in their life style and in their self-image. Even those who may want to give up the typical male stereotypes, who are tired of the "rat race" and of commuter life, may be emotionally unable to accommodate themselves to another way. Earth fathering will not hold long-term appeal as long as inner worth is judged by external success.

Even an unusual man who is able to face the loss of prestige and power that goes along with accepting earth roles has another issue to face. That is his partner. She must be able to accept some sky roles for herself and leave some earth parenting to him. Some men who are totally committed to becoming earth fathers will choose women who are eager to be full sky mothers, who will protect, provide and leave the nurturant functions to their husbands. These women want a career above all and will welcome a man who will take care of their children and thus free them from traditional female "bondage" in the home. Few women are comfortable with such a radical position.

It is one thing to want to get out of the routine of being a housewife and mother and another to be supplanted by a husband and see the children turn to him instead of her for nurturance. Society may see earth fathers as weak and impotent and call sky mothers hostile and castrating. Marital relationships have a hard time surviving a reversal in such deeply ingrained male-female differences. That is why we believe that the dyadic mode of parenting holds the greatest potential for both men and women. It allows for exploration of both sky and earth realms by both parents. As we shall see in later examples, dyadic parenting assumes a willingness to give up parts of oneself to the other. Dyadic parenting demands that the individual sacrifice his individuality and modify usual gender differences. It may require a great deal of psychological work for even the most committed and compatible couples to adjust to the demands of shared parenting.

Despite all the problems that have to be faced, fathering styles are changing. The new patterns are reflected in the expanding roles for expectant fathers, the increased participation of the father at the birth of his child, and the greater commitment to helping at home during the first few months of the infant's life. More evidence of the change comes from a small but significant number of men who seek to obtain custody of their children when they divorce. We also see some men who enter into a second marriage with the express purpose of "doing it right this time," which often means taking a larger nurturant role with the children.

The impact of these earth fathers is already being felt. There is a growing set of subliminal images being added to the modern parenting culture. Ads are beginning to use men to sell disposable diapers, for example (though the tone still tends to be condescending, referring to the occasion as ''mom's night out'' rather than assuming that men diaper routinely). One man, whose wife was nine months pregnant, came for brief therapy in order to work on a growing sense of unease about his parenting roles. He was troubled because he had only one positive image of himself as father: he kept thinking about carrying his child in a backpack in all the places where he now walked alone. He felt there should be something more. His own father had been out of the house most of the time. He could not remember any caring male behavior and was afraid he would not be able to go beyond his own father. The image of himself with his baby in the backpack seemed suspended in time, with no past and no future, a single element around which he hoped to build a meaningful relationship for his child and for himself.

Our society's laws hold a man responsible as a sky father only. His legal duty is to provide financially for his child. There are no obligations to create more meaningful social relations with his offspring. He will have to discover that kind of a role for himself.

Men receive little preparation for an earth fathering identity as children. Their first image will usually be that of sky father, for it is the standard of our society. Only a decade ago, men had little involvement with pregnancy or birth experience itself except to try to earn enough money to pay the bills. Pregnancy was (and is) a time when men began new businesses, took on extra jobs, and spent more time cultivating community and societal ties. Many wives were hurt by their husbands' apparent disinvolvement with their changing bodies. It was hard for them to understand that men were preparing for a very different role. All these outside activities were appropriate to their sky role, just as the woman's focus on diet, baby furniture, and childbirth were preparation for the earth role. The men were unconsciously laying the groundwork for their future relationship with child and family. The primary focus of that relationship lay outside the home.

Fathers who want a different fathering experience will need to begin as early as possible to forge new images of their own. They will be fortunate if they can find male earth parent images in their past. If not, they will have to take what they can from their mothers, teachers, friends, and love partners, and from the unconscious image of the primordial earth parent which lies within every man. The journey begins in pregnancy. It is a time of maximum creativity for the man as he prepares to become a father in his own image.

11

In the Beginning

The first definition of fatherhood in most dictionaries is biological: "One by whom a child is or has been begotten."[1] The man who provides half the genetic material is father to the child. For many men, especially those who will become traditional sky fathers, this definition of fatherhood is almost enough. At least until the earth phase of child-rearing is completed, his primary role will be to provide the mother with all she needs to make an appropriate environment for his child.

Much has changed. Men routinely go to childbirth preparation classes and attend the birth. Those who develop physical symptoms such as weight gain, abdominal swelling, or nausea, which mimic the symptoms of their pregnant partners, are as likely to be seen as involved as neurotic. Men are handling more child care in the postpartum months. Some of this change is the influence of the earth archetype on masculine psychology; some of it is demanded by women who refuse to be ignored in the sky world.

Since we want to see more nurturance and intimate caring in the parenting identity of fathers, we applaud every new level of male involvement in the pregnancy and birth experience, for it is then that the foundation of future parenting is really built. However, it is also important to recognize that the sky/earth split between men and women may not really be altered

---

[1]*The Random House Dictionary of the English Language*, ed. Jess Stein. New York: Random House, 1966, p. 445.

by the new involvement. It is hard to tell what each new facet of a man's involvement in pregnancy and childbirth actually means to him and to his wife. He may try out a childbirth class, a shopping trip to the baby furniture store, or diapering the newborn without fundamentally changing his attitude from the sky mode. He is "helping out" for his wife's benefit rather than taking on a new or meaningful identity for himself. For example, the husband who acts as a coach to his wife during labor and childbirth may be sharing the experience as profoundly as his biology will allow, or he may simply be playing out the traditional support role of the sky father. Is he there for his own experience or simply to help her? Similarly, the man who becomes intensely involved with the pregnancy experience may be forging a powerful beginning for his earth father role, or he may simply be trying to control his wife from his position as sky or even royal father. It is often difficult to tell what is really going on without interpreting the new behavior on a deeper level, the level of what it means to the family and, especially, to the father.

Let us explore some of the ways that men have traditionally acted during pregnancy, how they are changing their behavior, and what these changes may mean about developing the potential for earth fathering.

PREGNANCY

Fathering begins at the moment of conception even though the fact of the baby may remain unknown for weeks. Some men get most excited when they have the fantasy that their wife is going to conceive a child when they make love. Sometimes the fantasy becomes a reality; one man told us:

My own experience of that very special evening is still vivid. It was one of those occasions when our bodies were in harmony from the first caress, when passion and affection were perfectly intertwined. In the midst of the experience I became aware that this was more than superb sex, that I was simultaneously in the grip of an overwhelming force that had insured the survival of life from the time it began. I was creating life as a god creates life, a part of the creative force in the world. The experience of sex fused naturally with the awesome power of creativity. I possessed the pleasure and the power and was also possessed by them. The intensity increased beyond a level where words and recall can have any meaning. I do remember that with orgasm there was a sense of endless vistas, an infinity of space, which I was filling. It was not only the experience of sexual merger, but of merger with a great, steady power that was being unlocked for this life-creating occasion.

In those moments I was becoming a father, not in the sense of caring for a child or supporting a family, but in the sense of being creator of a universe.

This man, thanks to a combination of technology, a loving relationship, and luck, celebrated the conception of his child in the most profound manner imaginable.

But even with such luck, how can the celebration be continued beyond these first few moments for a male? Once he has participated in his supreme creative moment, the father may feel like the male praying mantis whose body is eaten by the fertilized female as the first nurturant act for their offspring. There is no longer anything he can do directly; he can only help the baby through helping the mother.

No matter how involved and interested a man may be in the process of pregnancy and childbirth, once fertilization occurs, the human male's main role feels like it is only to provide sustenance for the woman. True, his body is not actually consumed, but he may feel like a sacrificial figure whose only role is to provide food, clothing, and shelter for the incubating pair. If he accepts this view, he may become an onlooker, an outsider, a peripheral figure in the pregnancy while the creative action continues inside his partner's body. This movement toward the sky role in pregnancy may be accepted as natural and inevitable. Instead of fostering a link between creativity and fathering, pregnancy may be the time when a man begins to separate his own personal creativity from his fathering role. It may be his first experience of himself as a father who functions in the outside world.

Despite an increased recognition of the special characteristics of the ''pregnant'' male, our society still does little to acknowledge the biological creativity of men. It is hard for a potential earth father to feel the stirrings that link him to male fecundity. A man who is experiencing strong feelings about procreation may feel isolated from his male peers and drawn to women who are more comfortable with the emotions associated with fertility. If he suggests he is having symptoms that seem to go along with his wife's pregnancy, other men are likely to be embarrassed—although, if he talks with them long enough, he will probably discover that they do understand and have very likely been through it themselves.

Most men feel pride in what they have caused to be conceived, delight in lovemaking that has become more meaningful since the baby is involved, and joy at being able to take care of wife and children. But they simultaneously feel an impulse to escape the pressures of the pregnancy, an envy of the miracle going on in their wives, a jealousy of the baby for being so well protected, a fear that some danger may befall the helpless fetus, a frustration of wanting to take care of everything but of having nothing to do, and anxiety about whether they will be good fathers or be able to earn enough money to support the enlarged family.

The frustration and impotence experienced by pregnant men in general become particularly poignant when the decision is made to terminate the pregnancy. Abortion is often seen as an act performed only on the female body. Since therapeutic abortions are generally performed before the fetus has caused radical changes in the woman's appearance, before its movements can be felt or seen, few people acknowledge the act as the death of a child. Even fewer think abortion has any powerful meaning to the father. This is an oversight, for the feelings that have been stirred up in the expectant father are not shut down with an end to the actual pregnancy.

The effect of abortion on a prospective father is overlooked and even denied by professionals, both in the literature and in the many counseling agencies. Men are often excluded from the interviews at which the decision about abortion is made. When they are brought in, it is often with an attitude of blame.

All these attitudes are part of the fallacy that fatherhood begins after the baby is born, a fallacy that is part of the image of a sky father whose provider status is actualized only when there is objective need, "when the food bill increases." Men who are not helped to mourn over a miscarriage, an abortion, a stillbirth, or an early crib death are learning how to be even less involved as nurturant parents in the future. A male may experience the emotions of fatherhood as soon as he knows that he has created a living creature, even if that life ends before his child emerges from the womb. He may have no constructive outlet for those emotions and they may never even be acknowledged.

In *Pregnancy: The Psychological Experience,*[2] we document the panorama of experiences that accompany pregnancy for the man. As we point out, these changes are not simply the result of the different roles required of a man on the borderline of fatherhood. Pregnancy taps into the reveries from the past, from the little boy who dreamed of making a baby of his own only to discover that he could not. It also taps into dreams of the future and the question of whether or not he can deal with the approaching demands of family. At the same time, it challenges his adjustment in his day-to-day sexual and social relationship with his mate, who is also caught up in her own internal drama. It provides a laboratory for him to build a personal consciousness of his emerging fathering style as well as a relationship that will support that style.

Pregnancy is a huge event in the lives of both parents, but

[2]Arthur and Libby Colman, *Pregnancy: The Psychological Experience*. New York: Bantam Books, 1977.

the father's experience seems overshadowed by the obvious dramatic centrality of the mother. He may be in the throes of emotional turmoil, but compared to his mate, his changes seem minimal. He is caught up in the creativity which he has set in motion, but his place remains ambiguous. As pregnancy progresses, the father is poised in conflict between remaining with the developing family as a father and moving out to find other ways to express his creativity. The psychology of the pregnant father is ripe with this tension. At one extreme there are men who try to merge totally with the mother-to-be and even take on her pregnancy symptoms. At the other extreme there are men who escape from the developing family role by starting new ventures of their own, either alone, in the company of other men, or in relation to a nonpregnant woman. The ordinary pregnant man is filled with both tendencies.[3]

In a study of expectant fathers attending childbirth preparation classes, a psychologist learned that seventy-five percent of the men felt as though they shared in the pregnancy, as though it were happening to themselves as well as to their wives. Ironically, when their wives were asked whether or not they thought their husbands experienced the pregnancy that way, they generally answered no.[4] In other words, the wives were unable to perceive or accept the depth of involvement felt by their men. During pregnancy, women are busy going to the doctor, buying a wardrobe of maternity clothes, attending showers, identifying with the women in diaper ads, and thinking about the miracle within. Men have nowhere to turn, no

---

[3]Alan R. Gurwitt has traced the impact of pregnancy on a man's development in "Aspects of Prospective Fatherhood," *The Psychoanalytic Study of the Child* 31 (1976): 237–71. Building on this framework, James Herzog traces the stages of pregnancy, emphasizing the experience of men who are empathically attuned to their wives. "Biological changes occurring in the wife are lent to an expectant father and his attunement with her allows the father to use these compelling occurrences to regress, reassess, and reintegrate elements of his own caretaking line of development." "Patterns of Expectant Fatherhood," *Dialogue: A Journal of Psychoanalytic Perspectives* (1979), p. 64.
[4]John Wapner, "The Attitudes, Feelings, and Behaviors of Expectant Fathers Attending Lamaze Classes," *Birth and the Family Journal* 3 (1976):5–13.

one with whom to share their experience. Even their wives
don't acknowledge that anything is happening to them. No
wonder they turn to unconscious levels of communication.
Many experience the parts of themselves that feel involved in
pregnancy as exclusively female and unintegrated with their
self-image as male. It may be easier to unconsciously adopt
physical symptoms that mimic female body changes than to
find a more total way to express male involvement in
pregnancy.

Examples of psychological merger with the pregnant female
are known generically as *couvade* phenomena, an expression
derived from the French verb *couver,* ''to brood or hatch.''
The best known couvade behaviors take place during birth
itself. Nevertheless, there are many which occur during
pregnancy.

Many societies impose a series of rest and dietary prescriptions at specific times. Others forbid the husband from cutting
or killing anything. These are magical acts designed to deflect
dangerous evil spirits from attacking the vulnerable wife and
child. They prepare a man for a role as sky father, protector
of the family unit.

The Arapesh, as studied by Margaret Mead, represent a
society in which the father's creator role is continued into the
pregnancy. They believe that making a baby is a continuous
effort of the father and mother together:

> *The procreative task of an Arapesh father is not finished
> with impregnation. They have no idea that conception is
> a one-time event, that the father could go away and return
> nine months later to find his wife delivered of his child.
> They would consider such a form of parenthood impos-
> sible, and, furthermore, repellent. For the child is not
> the product of a moment's passion, but is made by both
> father and mother, carefully, over time. The Arapesh dis-
> tinguish two kinds of sex activity: play, which is all sex
> activity that is not known to have induced the growth of
> a child, and work, purposive sex activity that is directed
> toward making a particular child, towards feeding it and*

*shaping it during the first weeks in the mother's womb.
Here the father's task is almost equal to the mother's; the
child is the product of father's semen and mother's menstrual blood combined in equal parts to start, to form a
new human being.[5]*

Thus the Arapesh have developed a belief system which
allows the father to continue as a biologically powerful creator
even after conception has occurred. Like myths in which Zeus
takes over part of the female gestation and birth functions, the
Arapesh have transcended biological reality to keep the father
central during the pregnancy.

Most societies are like our own in not providing a role for
the father-to-be which reinforces his creator identity or helps
him make a bridge to nurturant fathering images. Some impose
prohibitions that keep him away from his wife throughout pregnancy. In societies which prohibit sexual relations during pregnancy, the father is often encouraged to take a new wife, if he
can afford one. Some impose sexual restraints on both father
and mother, but others, like parts of our own, don't expect the
man to be closely enough involved in the process of pregnancy
to want it to affect his sex life. Even the Arapesh, who participate so equally at the beginning of pregnancy, also share
the prohibition which is imposed at the end.

So many of the roles and behaviors given to pregnant men
by their cultures are variants of the father's attempt to stay
involved in a process which has moved beyond his control.
There isn't much difference between a man who refuses to use
a knife during the last six months of pregnancy and a man who
takes on another life insurance policy, or between a man who
goes off on a hunting trip to provide food for his new family
and a man who dramatically increases his work involvement
in order to bank money for the future education of his children.
All believe that their task in the family will be to protect it
from danger and provide for its security. They express their

---

[5]Margaret Mead, *Sex and Temperament in Three Primitive Societies*. New
York: Morrow, 1966, p. 31. Copyright 1935, 1950, 1963 by Margaret Mead.

involvement in the pregnancy in indirect ways which take them away from intimate relating with their family. They are being processed to become sky fathers.

Within our own pluralistic culture there is enormous variation in how a man's pregnancy is expressed, both within himself and through his actions. The only generalization really possible, besides the general bias towards sky images, is that no expectant father remains untouched by the nine-month experience. We have encountered men who have thrown themselves into activities like mountain climbing, auto mechanics, furniture building, and skiing, which require expensive equipment and training, only to have the interest evaporate soon after the child is born. Men who start a new business at this time are perhaps making a more productive investment in the future or developing other realms where they can become successful and productive.

Some American men have affairs during their wives' pregnancy and after the baby is born. Masters and Johnson report that twelve out of the seventy-nine men whom they questioned about pregnancy admitted to extramarital affairs at this time.[6] Some women have been trained to expect their husbands to redirect their sex lives; they may even be grateful that he has become less demanding, giving them more time and energy to devote to becoming a mother. But in our romantic love tradition, husband and wife expect to remain lovers. Marital infidelities are a source of terrible conflict, especially at this time, when they heighten the problems attendant with adjusting to the role of parents. A marriage may move inevitably toward divorce as a result of the unforgiven liaisons formed by a man who did not know how to stay in touch with his wife and express his sexual and masculine needs during pregnancy. Other marriages remain intact, but an atmosphere of tension and distrust has replaced the warm, loving home they had hoped to provide for their child. Sometimes the episode of infidelity does not occur in the first pregnancy, but rather comes with

---

[6]William H. Masters and Virginia E. Johnson, *Human Sexual Response*. Boston: Little, Brown, 1966, pp. 164–65.

the second or third. That particular baby becomes marked in the parents' mind, the unconscious recipient of blame and resentment, the inevitable scapegoat even for "good" parents who are not aware that they are thinking "if it weren't for you . . ."

There are many reasons why men run away from their pregnant wives and find respite with nonpregnant women. Some are jealous of the woman's creativity. Others are pushed away by wives who do not think pregnant women should make love. And many feel themselves that it is inappropriate to make love to a pregnant woman who is the embodiment of the Madonna. They may be disgusted by the body changes, by the huge breasts and the more engorged genitals; they may not like the smells. They may be frightened by the woman's new sexual demands. They may think she is fat and awkward. They may be afraid of hurting the baby or the mother-to-be. They may not know how to go about lovemaking when the traditional postures become awkward. New postures and, particularly, use of fondling, mutual masturbation, and oral-genital sex may be threatening to a man's need to feel in control of his sexual impulses. It may be particularly threatening and regressive for a man to resort to the kind of "necking" that he associates with naughty, adolescent behaviors and that he feels are inconsistent with the image of strong family man that he is trying to create. It may be the very pleasurable quality that is most frightening.[7]

On the deepest level, the fear is of the loss of their masculinity as they experience themselves merging with the pregnant woman who lies at their side night after night. Sexual function is often the first area to be affected by these unconscious conflicts. The wish to escape and to find an outlet for creative expression can focus in a new relationship. The man will be relatively free to do what he wants instead of feeling pressured to take on inescapable roles and responsibilities.

---

[7]For a discussion of the impact of pregnancy, birth, and the postpartum period on the sex lives of modern American couples, see Elisabeth Bing and Libby Colman, *Making Love during Pregnancy*. New York: Bantam Books, 1978.

Men who are living with a pregnant wife may dream about being pregnant, about giving birth, and about nursing a baby. Dreams of expectant fathers contain images of themselves with swollen bellies, large vaginas, and bizarre capacities to give birth through navels, ears, mouths, armpits, and anuses. In their sleep, men can admit their profound identification with the creative process of the female in ways that they would not dare acknowledge while awake. Conflict over accepting feminine parts of himself can push a man farther from his wife and family. When he is away from his wife, he may feel more secure about his own identity, his own masculinity.

Some American men now look for ways to become directly involved in the process of fathering, beginning in pregnancy. They are reading books and attending preparation-for-childbirth classes formerly reserved exclusively for women. They try to enter the experience in a variety of ways. There are even "expectant father groups" being formed in order to focus on the male experience without the inhibiting presence of pregnant females.

In our work with pregnant couples, we have found it important to understand all these reactions as attempts to find meaningful personal solutions to the conflict and paradox inherent in the experience of the pregnant father. The presence of a woman who is visibly creating a child affects a man's symbolic system as he attempts to discover new potentials within himself. The expectant father who expresses pregnancy symptoms or dreams is not just revealing his envy of his wife; he is also sharing in the process with her. He is using her as an intimate vehicle in his own creative search for a new identity. Arthur describes his own creative search for a new identity during three pregnancies:

My own response to our first pregnancy was to form a discussion group of "normal" pregnant women and transform it into a project which consumed me during the year surrounding the pregnancy and birth of our child. I have never known such an upsurge of creative energy as came to me during that period. Every week I would return home with tapes and notes full of the stories, dreams, and fantasies of "my" pregnant women. Libby would add her own experience. She became an invisible member of the group. I was present at the deliveries of each of the women in the group. Two of them occurred the same weekend as our own. It was only partially clear to me at that time that the choice of project and the energy with which I carried it out—two professional papers, computer programs of the group themes, radio and T.V. interviews, etc.—was both an attempt to compete with, even outdo, my wife and simultaneously to stretch my own creative potential to its absolute maximum. Simply put, it was my way of being pregnant.

And then, after the pregnancy was over, all that extra zest was suddenly gone. The envy, extra vitality, altered consciousness—all of it disappeared. The psychology of pregnancy no longer was so magical, and other subjects captured my attention. The papers I had written as part of the study, the piles of notes, tapes, and computer printouts that had been part of that work lay unused for over two years, until our second pregnancy began. Only then did I again find all of it meaningful. Again I wrote two papers in the field of the psychology of pregnancy.[8] Again I lost interest until our third pregnancy, when we found ourselves transformed into a baby-creating, book-creating juggernaut. Our book, Pregnancy: The Psychological Experience, *and our son Ari were born within months of each other.*

It was during that third and last pregnancy that I was able to collaborate fully with Libby in both earth and sky roles. That collaboration had its conflicts, but we were

---

[8]See Arthur D. Colman, "Psychological State during First Pregnancy," *American Journal of Orthopsychiatry* 39 (1960):788–97, and "Psychology of a First Baby Group," *International Journal of Group Psychotherapy* 21 (1971):74–83.

able to share the total experience from the male and the female side by merging and identifying with one another rather than competing. And strangely, with that integration, the experience of pregnancy did not fade after birth as it had before. Instead, the experience grew out into other areas of my life. Pregnancy remains the central metaphor for me, one to which I am drawn again and again in my psychotherapy work and in my writing. It is my metaphor for all beginnings and all creativity.

Sometimes I wonder whether becoming involved with pregnancy subtly downgraded all other creative endeavors, like academic research and teaching, in which I was not limited by my biology. Perhaps so, but I still count myself lucky to have found and expended so much energy to touch and understand the primal experience of creativity. Other areas felt grey for me, particularly when I was becoming a father. Everything else seemed derivative expressions of the more basic creative process which was being organically and psychologically expressed through the reality and the metaphor of pregnancy. If I were to compete with that, it would have to be without boundaries and without limits on myself. To distance myself from the pregnancy experience meant taking on another world and losing touch with my family.

Pregnancy is the first step in parenting and, like all beginnings, it has an extraordinary impact on the patterns that develop after the birth. Expectant fathers who find themselves emphasizing their protector and provider functions are laying the groundwork for sky father roles. It can be heard in the language they use to describe their feelings. A pregnant man will suddenly talk about his work as "creating a business for my new child" or "building a foundation for the child's education," or, more abstractly, helping to build a better society (school system, political party) for his child's future. Similarly, men who react to their pregnancy by becoming more interested in home, family, and nurturance, whose dreams and fantasies are full of fecund images, are moving in the direction of earth father roles. The form of fatherhood is created out of these tendencies and their integration with the woman's own needs as sky or earth parent.

In our own case, each pregnancy was a further step in the development of our parenting roles. Arthur was not content to be a boundary person in the family. His involvement with the first pregnancy was extreme. At first it was expressed in the work sphere, in the form of research and writing projects. He was hard put to integrate his experience of each pregnancy with the rest of his personal and professional life. Parenting too was more traditional, reflecting the culturally supported sky father/earth mother split. Increasingly through the last two pregnancies, however, both of us learned more about sharing these images between us rather than polarizing them. Our parenting style reflected this shift, and afterwards we began to function as dyadic parents more completely than we had before.

BIRTH

Birth is a moment of drama compared to the months of waiting that make up pregnancy. Suddenly there is more that can be done. Not surprisingly, this is as true for the male as for the female. For the woman, there is often a personal task of acquitting herself competently during labor and the birth. For a man, the emergence of his new child may be more central—how he supports his wife during the time of labor may or may not be important, depending on his relationship with her. Men need do nothing but wait for the moment of birth itself.

In fact, in most cultures men have a prescribed role during the labor, though not necessarily like that of the modern husband-labor coach. Some have customs which permit the father to go through the motions of labor in the birth house while the wife quietly gives birth to the baby elsewhere. Here the father is a decoy for the marauding evil spirits. He draws their attention away from the real thing through his dramatic mime of the birth. Tribes in upper Egypt prevent the father from even looking at the newborn until it is seven days old, for fear that he might be unwittingly carrying the evil spirit in his implements or on his person. Kurtatchi fathers in the Pacific islands must stop work, go into seclusion, and follow certain food prohibitions to protect the new child and the mother from evil forces.[9] It is almost as though the society is saying, "if you want to protect your wife and child, stay away." The parallel in our society still occurs when the father is excluded from the delivery room. He may spend his time pacing the floor in the waiting room or getting drunk at the bar across the street from the hospital; after the birth is completed, he proudly acknowledges his new role by passing out cigars and calling relatives and friends to announce the news. He remains peripheral to the birth experience but still uses it as the rite of passage for his fathering identity. A middle ground is found in one area of the Philippines where "the father of the first child is supposed to wash the rags which have been used in the delivery. This act means two things: (1) it is an admission that he is the true father of the child; (2) it is a sign that he has reached a stage of responsibility." This ritual provides a level of involvement which links him to his new role without making him central.[10]

There are many examples of childbirth customs in which the man more directly participates in helping his wife in the actual delivery process. The balance between indifference and excess is often delicate. At its best, modern childbirth preparation teaches the father how to be a labor coach without either feeling like a servant or taking control. He may learn how to massage his wife between and during contractions, help her with breathing techniques which maximize comfort, or focus her attention away from the urge to push.

---

[9]Edward Tylor, "Research into the Early History of Mankind" (London, 1865), cited by C. S. Ford, ed., in *Cross Cultural Approaches*. New Haven: Hraf Press, 1967, p. 199.

[10]Armandon J. and Paulay C. Malay, *Our Folkways* (Manila: Bookman, 1953), pp. 2–17; cited in *Birth*, by David Meltzer, editor. New York: Ballantine, 1973, p. 171. Copyright 1973.

Unfortunately, masculine involvement in this feminine function often leads to overcontrol, perhaps because this is one of the few functions in which the female is exclusively competent. Helping functions may hide aggression. Thus the Zina Cateco Indians in Mexico have the husband pull a cinch around his wife's waist to exert a downward pressure on the uterus and help expel the child, a practice which almost certainly is painful, counter-productive, and even dangerous.[11] Whenever men have dominated obstetrics, similar aggressive tendencies have appeared in the name of "good medical practice."[12] Routine forceps delivery and painful, unneeded spinal anesthesia are two modern examples of sky technology of no medical value that have violated women's bodies. The recent upsurge in *routine* monitoring procedures and caesarean births may well turn out to be yet another example of psychologically motivated control devices without medical rationale.

"Trained" husbands can become involved in ways that are supportive, not overbearing, and still useful in providing a male role that is valuable and affirming. The father can do a great deal technically to help a woman achieve a healthy, unmedicated delivery. However, these practical aids are sometimes seized upon as though they were magical rites. The father may secretly believe that his training has given him the ability to control the mystery of birth. Occasionally such beliefs (akin to pseudopregnancies in men), coupled with a poor rapport with their laboring wives, can actually impede the progress of labor, as in the case of Charles and Charlotte.

Charles came to a childbirth educator known for her positive feelings about home delivery. He told her he wanted to have his wife Charlotte deliver their second child at home because

---

[11]N. Fock, "South American Birth Customs in Theory and Practice," cited by C. S. Ford, op. cit., p. 201. For a careful account of the birthing practices of the Maya Indians in Yucatan, Mexico, including the husband's place as helper, see Brigitte Jordan, *Birth in Four Cultures*. St. Albans, Vermont: Eden Press Women's Publications, Inc., 1978.

[12]See G. J. Barker-Denfield, *The Horrors of the Half-Known Life*. New York: Harper Colophon Books, 1976; and Suzanne Arms, *Immaculate Deception*. Boston: Houghton Mifflin Co., 1975.

the hospital had made such a mess of things with their first child. He described Charlotte's first labor as long and slow. Finally, after twenty-four hours of little action, Charles went out for supper. While he was gone, perhaps not totally accidentally, he wife's bag of waters broke and her contractions suddenly became much stronger. When Charles returned, Charlotte was no longer relaxed and comfortable. She was thrashing around in agony. He tried and tried "to get her under control," but no matter what he said or did, she could not get comfortable. Finally he agreed to medication, although even that did not seem to get Charlotte to relax fully. Charles believes that if he had never left his wife's side, things would never have "gotten out of control." He may be right. However, there is another possibility implicit in his description of feeling impotence watching the doctor, the "other man," take over in the hospital.

Ultimately, every man is impotent when his wife is giving birth. His body cannot do the job for her. He may be able to help, but he cannot control the complex physiological progression of birth. Charles's insistence on "control" may have prevented his wife from letting her body enter the process of labor. Charles was well intentioned, but it is likely that he hindered more than he helped.

Over thirty years ago, men in the United States were completely separated from the actual birth experience. The rationale provided by the medical profession was that fathers are inept and incompetent in the labor and delivery rooms, prone to fainting at the first sight of blood, and unable to bear the sight of their wives in discomfort. Certainly there must have been a few cases to begin such a myth, but we know now that it was a myth, one perpetuated by the predominantly male obstetricians who felt the threat of another male entering their inner sanctum and watching them operate on women's bodies. Ultimately, this myth allowed male doctors to dominate the birthing females.

Since fathers have been coming into delivery rooms, few have acted in any but the most helpful and joyous ways. An occasional man is overly aggressive toward the childbirth professionals or may try to dominate his wife for psychological reasons, but even in these situations it is often because the husband is intensely involved and well intentioned. Sensitive helpers can usually reeducate such a man to help him become comfortable with the people around him. Birth can be an exciting, wonderful moment for a man. He can be his wife's most intimate and sensitive companion. In addition to helping her to a better experience, he can have a profoundly meaningful event of his own.

The moment of birth is the most obvious, concrete time to celebrate the act of creation. The event can become the "sacred time" during which the more mundane, profane aspects of pregnancy can be forgotten and even the practical difficulties of parenting do not yet need to be faced. The deepest meaning of life creation can be fully experienced in a moment set aside as special.

Poet David Meltzer described the birth of his child in mystical terms:

> *The baby came forth in a moment of silence that was filled with the roar of the universe. I swear I heard the earth moving on its axis in those final moments when the baby's head was pushing thru (sic). As I reached to turn the body so the shoulders would not cause a tear, the light in the room was of a quality I have never known. It was a light fashioned in facsimile of it: in paintings, ikons, barely described in tracts and texts of great inner journeys.*[13]

Many others not as articulate as Meltzer have described similar transcendent feelings when they first heard their wives were pregnant and in flashes during the pregnancy. But for men who experience the birth in a setting which allows emotional participation, such ecstasy is not unusual.

Even while recognizing the incredibly profound experience of most men at the moment of birth of their own child, we must also point out the difficulties implicit in choosing birth

---

[13]David Meltzer, *Birth*, op. cit., p. 296.

as a focus for celebrating fatherhood. Birth is the supreme moment of uniquely female creativity, an act which no male can ever duplicate. The major triumph of the childbirth education movement has been to free women from the domination of male professionals and the drugs and technology they used to control the female body. Fathers have benefited from the changes. The father can participate as a helper; he may guide the mother's breathing, rub her back, ward off intrusive hospital staff, or translate her needs to a busy obstetrician. In the delivery room or particularly at a home birth, he may even be able to perform more specific acts in relation to the child, such as "catching" the baby or cutting the umbilical cord. These are all acts of some practical and also symbolic importance, but they fall short of a celebration of the father's role as creator. To be a rite of passage, a creative celebration should dramatize the real roles and relationships of the future. Mother and child play amazing roles in the process of birth. Even the doctor, no matter how he tries to insure his preeminence, is all but superfluous in a normal delivery. If a man has already celebrated his role as father creator, then the birth can be a confirmation of the miracle he has wrought. But if the moment of birth itself is the initial defining ceremony for a paternal identity, the father is likely to experience himself as peripheral to the experience. If he takes on the duty of cutting the cord, he is perhaps accepting his role as the one who will lead the child out from its mother's arms into the world beyond the home. If he "catches" the baby and hands it over to the mother, he is symbolically saying, "Here, I will always protect the child and bring it back to you."

No matter how involved a father becomes in the birth experience (and we fully support his total commitment), he can only be a guide, a helper, a support to his wife. She is in the center of the stage. At the time of the birth, his role must be on the boundary of the experience. He can protect and aid, but she must do.

For some men there is a deep hurt in this limit on the creator roles. They may still harbor an unconscious fantasy of their own totipotentiality in the sexual and reproductive realms. In men coming from special family backgrounds, this reaction is understandable. A lay midwife whose son accompanied her to several home births told us about her son's dismay when he learned that he would not be able to give birth to a baby. He cried and refused to believe the unfair fate he was told was his. Birth was highly valued in the world in which he lived. It was painful to be excluded from a central role in that act. All men share this pain to some extent, for few persons can easily accept their own limitations, especially those that are inborn. A man who is a partner in the birth experience must face his limits in the most graphic way. It is no wonder that so many men find it difficult to find a secure role at the birth. Perhaps the ambivalence of some men to partake as fully as they are allowed in the delivery of their children is not simply because of disinterest or squeamishness. Perhaps, consciously or unconsciously, they understand that only a very limited aspect of their fathering role is allowed expression at this time, one that need not represent the ultimate expression of their paternity.

Experienced fathers who want to expand their own fathering identity beyond the traditional sky roles often need to reinterpret how they wish to take part in the birth. For example, William had coached his wife through labor with their first two children. Young and eager to help, but also feeling guilty that he spent so many hours a week at work and so few at home, he had felt he should do whatever his wife wanted, for after all, wasn't she in charge of babies? But when their second child was eight months old, he took six months off from work "to get to know the family" and really share in parenting. Two years later he learned he would become a father yet again—this time he understood that the children were *his* as well as hers. He told his wife he did not want to be labor coach again and that she should find an experienced woman to do the job. He wanted to be completely free to celebrate the birth as father and husband, not as technician or helper.

Sometimes it seems as if our culture has turned full circle in the past decade in redefining fathers' roles during the birth experience. Before, they were excluded from entering the labor room at all; now they are expected to play important roles during the delivery. For some couples this means sharing entirely in an experience without considering the depth of their commitment to one another and the kind of relationship they hope to develop as parents. We have been impressed with the number of couples who become involved in childbirth preparation and birth only to break up soon after the "high" is over and the need for real commitment and sharing as parents begins. In retrospect, many of these couples seem to have been using the pregnancy to cement a relationship that was already crumbling. But birth, like sex, cannot keep a couple together if they don't have a meaningful relationship. On the contrary, both are ecstatic moments which force individuals to come to grips with what is really important to them. As one man expressed it, "It was such a wondrous thing, watching my son being born and being a part of it, that I knew I couldn't go on pretending to love when it wasn't really there. I kept hating myself for faking. Life is too precious. My wife and I—and especially my son—deserve more."

One of the hazards for men and women who hope to enrich their lives together by celebrating rites of passage such as birth in nontraditional ways is that the outcome for any individual may be unexpected. Thus the search for more involved fathering inevitably carries with it a parallel search for personal meaning in all relationships. A man may find that his experience during this time carries him away from a traditional relationship with his wife and child. He may want to seek ways to be a father which will keep alive the growth he felt during pregnancy and birth, ways not supported by the usual male parenting role or by the assumptions of his wife. Men who find their lives changed by involvement in the birth process (rather than by their exclusion) are a new breed, one we can expect to see more of as earth father consciousness grows.

Even when a man is involved in the entire pregnancy, the birth may illuminate his future fathering image in subtle ways he may not have expected. The couple in the next example are trying to forge a family unit based on principles of "equality," paying more attention to similarities than differences. Their relationship, their commitment to each other is deep and secure. The birth experience was as special for the father as he had hoped, but not in the way he expected.

Bob and Barbara both have professional careers that they consider important, but they are both willing to make sacrifices in order to have a family. Their pregnancy was planned; they both knew exactly when the baby was conceived. They shared in the pregnancy, both going to preparation classes, both reading up on the topic, and both working on the posture and relaxation classes. They took up yoga together because they felt those exercises could benefit the pregnancy. They had read that orgasm occasionally initiated labor, so as the due date approached, they began to make love more often in a more leisurely way than usual. Their first few attempts were successful as lovemaking sessions, but did not start labor. Then, a few days after the due date, contractions started after an orgasm and continued at regular intervals. Bob was very proud and excited; he felt as though he had done it, as though he had participated in a very real way. He stayed with Barbara in the hospital, helping her in every way he could. When she tensed up and forgot her breathing, he whispered in her ear and told her how beautiful she was and how proud he was of her for doing this incredible thing. He wiped her sweaty brow and fed her ice chips. When she wanted to get up and walk around, he let her lean heavily on his shoulders during contractions. Bob remarked afterwards:

> *I was surprised in the delivery room. She wasn't looking at me any more. Before, she'd been counting on me for every breath, but when the baby was actually coming out, it was as though she cared more about that than about me! And the nurse was the one telling her when to push. I felt really out. I'd gone through all that, and here I was with nothing to do. They didn't need me anymore.*

> *Then I started to look at Barbara in a different way. She was my woman, and she was making all these incredible noises. Like some gigantic orgasm. Her whole body was*

involved in this process. And I saw the baby start to emerge. I had wanted to catch it, but I saw how careful the doctor was being. I saw how he held it just so, how he knew just what to do. He gave her to me first. The excitement! I could have leaped with joy. It was my daughter, and she was the most incredible creature I have ever seen. I would be her father. Barbara had done a good job, but I couldn't focus on her anymore, only on my daughter. We needed each other. All that time I had been preparing for becoming a father and didn't really know it.

Bob and Barbara both took off two months from work to try to share equally in the earliest adjustments to parenting. After that, they both worked half-time. Their daughter is only three months old, so it is too early to tell what long-term patterns will evolve, but through the pregnancy and birth and even into the earliest postpartum months, Bob worked out ways to stay as intimately involved as possible in becoming a parent. He says that he did have trouble trying to connect what he was doing with what he knew about "fathers." He joined a men's discussion group and admits that a lot of his support came from the feeling that he was a pioneer, a man breaking through new frontiers of how to father.

EARLY EARTH FATHERING

Our culture tends to underestimate the possibility for a father's involvement in the very earliest months of the child's life. Fathering does not need to begin when the child becomes "civilized"—that is, when it can walk, talk, play ball, and be a buddy. On the contrary, earth fathering begins with diapering, cuddling, and cooing. The father's early involvement with his offspring may be an incredibly creative time for both, once the father is able to value process over product. Is teaching a boy to play ball really more important than being a part of his first efforts at crawling or feeding himself? Obviously not, once out-worn cultural expectations are laid to rest.

There is some evidence that a father's early interaction with his newborn is a critical releaser of parenting impulses which may otherwise not surface until the child is mobile and verbal. Martin Greenberg and Norman Morris have studied fathers' potential for involvement with their newborns.[14] They coined the term *engrossment* to describe what they saw: the men were engrossed; they had "feelings of preoccupation, absorption, and interest in their newborn. When the father is engrossed in his individual infant, the infant has assumed larger proportions for him. In addition, it is suggested that the father feels bigger, and that he feels an increased sense of self-esteem and worth when he is engrossed in his infant."

These investigators feel that engrossment is a basic, innate potential among all fathers, one which is fostered and activated by the earliest possible visual and tactile contact with the newborn. Their interviews suggest that those fathers who were already ambivalent toward becoming fathers could be pushed "over the threshold of their negativity through such early involvement." Many of the men they studied were unprepared for their positive reactions, for they had been primed for the cultural stereotype. They thought they would not be interested in the child until it grew up. One man said, "I thought if it was going to be a boy and everything was going to be great, we could go out and jump around and play about together. I was thinking about eighteen months, two years, two and one half years, then we'd start to have a relationship. And I thought for the first eighteen months it would be for the wife and everything would be fine for her and I'd just take it easy. But it wasn't like that at all. It was completely different. The kid was born—and I was there—and I really had a strong feeling toward her." He had had no conscious image of the earth father within himself, no way to anticipate the rush of nurturant,

[14]Martin Greenberg and Norman Morris, "Engrossment: The Newborn's Impact upon the Father," *American Journal of Orthopsychiatry* 44 (1974):520–31.

protective, loving feelings that were evoked by his own new child. He thought only mothers felt such things.

Because infants characteristically remain relaxed and alert for the first hour or so after birth (if the mother has not been medicated) and then fall into a deep sleep for a few hours, the first moments after birth usually are a good time for the father as well as the mother to interact with their offspring. There is experimental confirmation of parents' observations that a baby is preprogrammed to be more interested in the human face than any other object. More specifically, babies seem to prefer direct eye contact to more general looking. If the father presents his face, the unmedicated newborn will reward him with rapt attention, for he is giving his child the visual treat that the infant wants most.

Most investigators who have watched both mothers and fathers interacting with their infants during the first few days after birth have found no significant behavior differences between fathers and mothers except the ones directly linked to nursing. For example, Parke observed that both parents seemed equally able to experience intense bonding, to feel the rush of attachment. When he observed the triad, the mother and father and baby together, he found that "the father tends to hold the infant nearly twice as much as the mother, vocalizes more, touches the infant slightly more, smiles at the infant significantly less than the mother." Fathers are clearly capable of being profoundly involved with their newborn babies. Their dominance while with the mother does not necessarily indicate that they are the more interactive, nurturant earth parent, but rather that the mother withdraws to let the father get to know the child. "In this triadic interaction the mother's overall interaction declined"—that is, declined from the intensity of interaction she had when alone with the child.[15]

Objective evidence demonstrates again and again that fathers

---

[15]R. D. Parke and S. O'Leary, "Father-Mother-Infant Interaction in the Newborn Period," *The Developing Individual in a Changing World*, Vol. 2 of *Social Environmental Issues*, K. Riegel and J. Meacham, eds. The Hague: Mouton, 1975.

can interact as much (and as well) as mothers in the early hours and days of their children's lives. But what happens to the family when it is at home, away from the eyes of researchers? How much time do fathers spend with their infants? The answer seems to be shockingly little. One study recorded infant vocalizations through twenty-four-hour periods. They found that the fathers had few verbal interactions with the babies—only about 37.7 *seconds* per day![16] Middle-class American men don't seem to spend much time with their infants. But the situation is not much different in other societies. Cross-cultural analysis has shown most of them have minimal contact between fathers and their very young children.

> If "regular close relationship" between father and child is equated with "half or less of time" spent together by mother and child, then 4% of fathers are close to infants, compared with 98% of mothers. In early childhood, 9% of fathers are close, compared with 66% of mothers. These distributions show an extreme discrepancy between maternal and paternal proximity in infancy that lessens slightly in early childhood.[17]

A suggestive finding in another cross-cultural study was that there is an inverse relationship between the degree of warfare in the society and the amount of contact between fathers and their infants.[18] Peaceful societies are characterized by more father-infant contact; warlike societies minimize father-infant contact. Perhaps the current movement towards more nurturant fathering in our own culture is dependent upon our current period of relative peace. Perhaps, too, future generations with stronger memories of earth fathering will value continued peace.

---

[16]F. Rebelsky and C. Hanks, "Fathers' Verbal Interaction with Infants in the First Three Months of Life," *Child Development* 42 (1971):63–68.
[17]Mary Maxwell West and Melvin Konner, "The Role of the Father: An Anthropological Perspective," *The Role of the Father in Child Development*, Michael E. Lamb, ed. New York: John Wiley, 1976, p. 202.
[18]Ibid., p. 197.

Most fathers continue to play traditional roles. Nevertheless, we have known many men who wanted to be as involved as possible in the care of their infants from the earliest moments. This has meant different things in different families. At its most extreme, it has meant that the father wanted to be the primary parent and assumed full earth parenting responsibilities for the child. For example, a man we will call Jim learned when he was twenty-one that his girlfriend of the past few months was unexpectedly pregnant. She assumed that she would have an abortion, but he urged her not to. Instead, he proposed, and they were married almost immediately.

Jim had not realized that he wanted to have a baby until he heard about the pregnancy. He was overwhelmed by the strength of his paternal emotions. He certainly could not afford to support a wife and child, since he was a full-time student; he did not know the mother very well; and yet he could not let her have an abortion. Instead, he promised her that he would assume responsibility for the baby so that she could return to work. When they could afford a babysitter he would finish his classes.

Jim's wife found that she did not like mothering. For a year and a half, she worked while he took care of the child and continued his studies on a part-time basis. Then she filed for divorce and asked Jim to leave. He was shocked—after all, it was *his* baby. But mothers are awarded the children as a matter of course in most divorce courts, and so it turned out in this one. Jim had visiting rights on weekends, but that was all. He ached for his son but saw no solution. He quickly finished his education and started his career. Soon after he had become established on his first job, his ex-wife suggested that he should become the primary parent again. He immediately accepted.

Jim found that it was more difficult to parent while attempting to advance on the job than it had been as a part-time student. He felt constant tension between his two worlds. When he worked overtime, he worried about his son. When he took off from work to be with his child, he worried about his job. He continued in this unresolved way for several years until he met another woman. He was about to marry her and take a new job (the perfect job he had been dreaming of all his life) when he realized what was happening. If he married and took this new job, he would be working fifty or more hours a week. His new wife would be the one doing the real parenting of his son. Was that what he really wanted? He remembered his first reaction when he learned about the pregnancy. He still did not know why, but he knew that he wanted to take care of that "baby" (who was now six years old). He turned down the job and postponed the marriage. He felt that he had almost taken part in a script of manhood written for someone else. He had always assumed he should advance in his career, but when he really confronted the parental consequences of this commitment, he realized it was not what he had wanted at all. He had been living with the conflict between earth and sky since he resumed caring for his son; finally it was resolved. Earth won.

Jim is unusual but not unique. Men are trying to be important nurturers during the first year; some are actually taking the primary responsibility. It is still very unusual for a man to be the earth parent and also live harmoniously in his marriage. Divorces such as Jim's are not uncommon. Neither are sexual difficulties. We know a family who had adapted well to an earth father/sky mother split in all areas except the sexual. The father, Ed, became impotent during the pregnancy and remained that way until he finally decided to go back to work (when the baby was ten months old). Ed was in his forties. He had been a traditional sky father in an earlier marriage and had hoped to create a more nurturant pattern this second time around. He believed strongly in the role reversal. His wife Peggy was happy with her work and particularly enjoyed her business trips, from which she would return refreshed and ready to help out with child-care chores. Both partners were very upset about their sexual problem. They had been married for five years before the baby was born. Sex had always been especially good and meaningful. They were amazed at the impact of parenting and work roles on their intimate lives together, but they felt sure that it was related to Ed's feeling too much like a "mother" and Peggy's feeling too much like a "father."

It would be a mistake to see Ed and Peggy's experiment as a total failure. They both learned a great deal about each other, and about the images they needed to have to keep their relationship erotic. Ed also had the opportunity to test out his earth father potential. We imagine that his future relationship with his child will have benefited even if he never returns to a wholly nurturant stance again.

The urge to celebrate fatherhood in traditional sky ways may be very strong, even in highly unconventional men. We have watched artists become advertising designers and poets become administrators as if to assert their masculinity when their child is born. But we have also known men who have been spurred by the birth to a commitment to be earth or dyadic fathers and who have stuck to it despite the social and personal pressures toward conformity.

In the following passage, Arthur describes his own feelings the night after our daughter Shoshana was born.

Throughout the pregnancy I had tried to be as involved as possible. My research on a pregnancy group had helped, as did my "fraternal" relationship to the obstetrician and the pediatrician. As an M.D., I was comfortable in the labor and delivery rooms at the hospital. No one thought of keeping me out—not because I was the father, but because I was a doctor. (This was 1965.) We insisted in advance that we would leave the hospital within a few hours of the birth, and again it was my medical degree that earned their cooperation.

When we arrived home, I nurtured Libby and our tiny daughter. I remember feeling profound joy and peace that first night; I was a true father in every sense. Lib was asleep in our bed and Shoshi was in her crib in the living room near me. Then she began to cry, the marvelous ululations of the newborn that reverberate with both life and loss. I wanted to comfort her, ostensibly to let Libby regain her strength after the long labor, but also to take care of her myself. I was bare to the waist because it was a warm August evening. I took a bottle of sugar water and gently touched the plastic nipple to Shoshi's lips while I cuddled her to my chest.

She was quiet for a moment and then began to wail. I tried the bottle and my chest again and again, but with no better effect. My breasts ached. It was probably the fatigue and emotion, but for a moment I was sure that I had milk there for her. I let her lips touch my nipple. She nuzzled slightly and then wailed even louder. Libby was obviously awake by now (she claims to have wakened at the first squeak) and was smiling at me. She held out her arms for our infant and in a moment the crying had stopped as Shoshi found a "real" nipple.

It was a hard fantasy to let go, a fantasy in which I could do everything and be everything as a parent. I was depressed for a long while. It was hard to start off second-best. I'm sure it took a lot more courage to stay in there at home than it had to be the father-protector at the hospital. There, I had known my way around. At home that night I felt like I had a "disability."

Every man with earth father ambitions will face similar real and imagined inadequacies, especially if there is a breast-feeding mother in the family. One father told us of the embarrassment he felt at being the only father in a babysitting co-op. The mothers rarely included him in their kaffeeklatches, which meant that he missed out on the valuable information about earth parenting that was exchanged in these informal get-togethers. He found that the other fathers were even more uncomfortable with him. He provoked guilt in most; a few questioned his masculinity or intimated that he was after their wives. The implicit question from both the men and the women was, would a "real man" actually choose to do the child care while his wife worked?

If a man can transcend the pressures to conform to traditional male patterns, the rewards are rich indeed. Couples who are able to share early parenting find that they come through the childbearing year with a greater sense of intimacy than they have ever had before. The inevitable fatigue, frustration, and confusion that come with trying to care for a young baby seem less painful when they are shared. The father cannot project all his negative feelings onto his wife. He must accept equal (or more) responsibility for successes and failures in the day-to-day crises of life with an infant.

Wives of men who have shared the early parenting have told us how important it was to them. They say that their own mothering felt more legitimate because their partners accepted its importance, too. One woman, Alice, explained how she felt when, after four months of dyadic parenting, her husband returned to work:

> *All of a sudden I was the suburban housewife, and it was very hard for me, and for Alan, too. He missed the baby terribly and was feeling guilty. It also accelerated my interest in doing something else. Sometimes I feel as isolated here as I did in the Peace Corps where I was the only English-speaking person within a hundred miles. I mean, I look forward to the mailman. It's absurd.*

Alan and Alice had always been extremely close. They remained that way for the first four months after the baby was born. It was only when they shifted into distinctly different parenting roles that they began to feel distant from each other. Alan had felt that he preferred the dyadic parenting also, but that he was forced back to a full-time job by economic considerations. Once he had returned to the sky world, he felt strongly that Alice should stay at home full-time. If he could not be with the baby, at least she should be there for him. Ironically, his absence made her want to join him in the sky world instead of taking his place in the earth world.

The practical realities of life require that someone earn a living for the family. The father has been carefully socialized toward this provider role, and society still discriminates in his favor in many work settings. Increasingly, women need and want to work too, even during their childbearing years. So it may be practical for men to take time off around birth to learn about their infant, if only to establish a viable sharing pattern for the future. It has been our observation that fathers who are able to take off some time, even if it is only a week or two, establish a firm connection with the earth world. They remain engaged with their children and do not feel that they have to wait for them to become verbal or play ball or be ready to apply to college before they can be intensely involved.

When a man is able to take a month or so at the birth and actually uses that time to participate fully in the family (rather than to hide away in the den or to go off fishing), he is likely to continue to be an involved husband and father who will be able to complement his wife's parenting, even if he returns to work full-time to the sky world afterwards. When a mother knows that there is a second person who is fully competent to care for her children, she, too, is much freer to pursue her own interests. We know from our own lives that Arthur's early involvement in pregnancy and infancy with each child was the cornerstone for greater and greater sharing as a nurturant parent. Equally important was Libby's feeling that since Arthur is so involved in earth activities, she should be involved in sky activities. Since he shares domestic responsibilities with her, she wants to share financial responsibilities with him.

It is hard to fill the role of expectant or new father when the landmarks for that role are virtually nonexistent. Society's stereotype of the man who goes out in the dead of night for pickles and ice cream or who loses his way en route to the hospital or who faints in the delivery room or who is frightened to touch the fragile newborn are no help. They are being challenged now, but the new images are still hazy and often uncomfortable. A father may not want to become a priest officiating at a communal birth ceremony, nor a hero fighting with hospital personnel to assure a place for himself in the delivery room. He needs an image suited to his personal style and family relationship.

What he learns about himself during conception, pregnancy, birth, and early parenting is not simply to provide a preparation for parenting or a reexamination of his marital relationship. What he learns will affect his personal growth irrespective of the living product of those experiences. What is tapped is the inner image of his own creativity, and the imprint of that reawakening will be felt in all his future endeavors.

A man's reaction to his expectant-father role is also practice for his future identity as a social father. His role as creator is assured; now he must go on to define a way to actually function in relation to the new life. His experience in the pregnancy is linked to his future as a parent and to his past as a son. During his pregnancy, he may find that, no matter how hard he tries, he cannot find a way to be involved. He can blame job pressure, outside interests, difficulties in the marriage, but whatever the cause, he feels the increasing distance. Conversely, he may find that no matter how hard he tries to escape, circumstances keep drawing him closer and closer to his expectant family. He may want to blame external circumstances for the path he takes, and he may be partially correct, yet he is also likely to find, if he looks hard and deep enough, that he himself is determining the direction in which he is moving.

When a baby is born, the man has done more than create a child; he has also created a father in himself and participated in the creation of a mother in his wife. While the role is still new, he may find himself deluged with conscious and unconscious images of what he will be as a father. He must sort through these images and make choices about his own potential to fulfill each possibility. Decisions about what kind of father to become may begin before the first pregnancy and continue to be made well after the last child is born. To some extent, each man continues to create himself as a father throughout his life, as he interacts with his children and makes choices about his relationship to his family. He takes his first step onto that path of fatherhood with the creation of his child, the choices around pregnancy and birth, and (if he decides to become an earth parent) with the beginning of an active nurturant role with his newborn.

12

Earth Fathering

The family is the most conservative element in any culture. Traditional patterns die hard. Couples attempting to abandon the ubiquitous sky father/earth mother split still face social disapproval, though less than ever before. Yesterday's unconventional parenting patterns are gradually becoming acceptable today. Especially in the early months, fathers and mothers will find many of their peers interested in and supportive of nontraditional child-care styles, especially those that include more involvement for the father.

Young adults who thrive on disputing the old ways may actually gain strength from whatever superficial disapproval they feel from their parents and relatives. They will feel like constructive revolutionaries who are forging a better life for the next generation. Older couples may feel more identified with established customs and more sure of their own unique life style. They may feel secure in creating a nontraditional pattern with or without the support of their extended family. Nevertheless, it is common for couples to compare themselves with others and to be aware of the approval or disapproval of others.

The research findings reported in Chapter 11 are generally supportive to those couples who wish to break with tradition. They imply that men can be involved and nurturant parents. However, social conditioning is not easily changed by research data, or even by the conscious desire to be different. The ways of our parents and the ways we were parented become reac-

tivated when we become parents ourselves. They are represented within our unconscious. The inner voice of our paternal
figures reach us from our childhood. To resist, or better, to
integrate these aspects of our personality with newer dimensions of parenting behavior, is a formidable job that requires
a great deal of inner psychological work.

We have found that many of the couples who use the popular
culture and their own rebellious energy to develop a new approach to parenting during pregnancy and the early months of
infant care have difficulty sustaining their commitments once
the newness wears off. Without this creative energy, the conflict between rejected but still emotion-laden images and the
new, tentative patterns can erode self-confidence. What begins
as an adventure may, after a year or so, seem difficult and
unstable. Those ancient parental voices and conservative societal traditions have a way of counterattacking when least
expected.

One couple we studied illustrates this pattern. Al and Ellen
met in a college community in the early 1960s. They explored
the various forms of life style around them and considered
these adventures as much a part of their education as political
science or English literature. They remained close to each other
while enjoying other sexual relationships and despite periodic
break-ups. They both felt their relationship was stronger and
more meaningful because of sexual experimentation. By the
time they married, they had worked out a code of sexual mo-
rality that combined occasional, casual liaisons with their
preeminent commitment to each other.

Both partners wanted children and assumed that they would
be able to work out a single standard of parenting which would
mirror the kind of equality they insisted upon in their relationship. At the time of their pregnancy, both went to graduate
school, and both held jobs. Household chores and financial
responsibilities were divided equally. They were very optimistic about their chances for creating new parental roles because they felt they had successfully developed and maintained
new sexual patterns. They had in effect decided to be dyadic

parents and felt they had the personal experience and the relationship to make it work.

Ellen and Al went to childbirth education classes together. He was present at the delivery and shared in most of the early infant care. He could not nurse his new son—he, Ellen, and their friends often joked about that—but he did do everything else and was so involved in the infant that when Al's parent's came to visit, he experienced a sense of superiority over his own father, who readily admitted that he had done little of the kind of intimate fathering that he saw in his son. But Al was surprised to experience another feeling also, one of hollowness and ahistoricity, of estrangement from his father, which increasingly became a dominating emotion as his first son grew and his second was born.

Six years after the birth of their first child, Al and Ellen had been divorced for one year. They were in the process of fighting over custody of their children in court. Both saw this as the ultimate disaster in their experiment to create a new form of family. They told the following story.

They had continued to share the work of parenting without any division along sex lines, but it had never actually felt really equal to Al. Despite his intense political convictions about what the "new" father should find meaningful, he experienced his day-to-day parenting as increasingly empty. He felt "castrated" by the enforced blurring of fathering and mothering roles. He felt jealous of Ellen's breast-feeding and of her pregnancy. These things were not equal. She kept something special as part of her femininity; what did he have that was special as part of his masculinity? He said it all might have been worth it if he had experienced an inner sense of growth as a father. Instead, he found his fantasies turning toward filling the kind of roles that he had seen his own father perform when he was a child. His mind would dwell on the prerogatives of male authority; he even imagined himself in a comfortable chair by the fire while his child brought him his slippers and his wife prepared his dinner. Much to his chagrin, he felt envy of his own father's "old fashioned" pattern, the pattern he had consciously rejected.

While Al felt frustrated, Ellen blossomed. She clearly appreciated the time away from mothering, saying it made her a better mother when she returned. She had the best of both worlds. Al felt as though he had the worst of both worlds, as though he was sacrificing himself for her. Most irrational of all, he felt that his new kind of fathering roles would make his sons think less of him, that they would not respect him as a man!

The confusion around parenting roles soon spread to the rest of the marriage. Al resented Ellen's time away from home, particularly her sexual infidelities. Where before her occasional affairs had stimulated his erotic appetites, now he felt cuckolded. He pictured himself "minding the kids so that she could screw." He began to pick up other women without telling her, nursing the unnecessary secret against her.

Eventually Al found another woman who had more traditional values. She had children of her own and wanted a father for them. She was willing to care for the children and expected him to provide for them. Divorce ensued; Al and Ellen agreed upon equal custody.

Parenting was not the only issue upon which this marriage foundered, but it seems to have been a major one. Their prior creativity in sexual and relational areas was unequal to the challenge of living with an invented system of parenting. It was hard to maintain a pattern which had no links to the parenting which they had experienced as children. Al attempted to establish himself as part earth father, part sky father, the kind of integrated man he thought he wanted to be. He worked to define the kind of relationships he wanted to have with his wife and children. But he was working against forces inside himself, forces that he never fully confronted. He felt he could be different from (and better than) his own father, but he found himself more anxious than triumphant. Ellen's freedom to be more than a mother did not enhance Al's security as a father. He even found that the closeness with his son made him feel weak and empty. When he tried to view himself through the eyes of his son, he felt inadequate. He was surprised to find that the son treated him with more joy when he was with him less. His attraction to a woman who wanted to be a traditional earth mother allowed him to become a more conventional sky father and solved his phychological crisis.

Men and women like Al and Ellen, who seek new roles in their families, need to find images that are deep enough to satisfy their unconscious needs. The conscious choice to act contrary to old patterns is not enough. A person must have a positive alternative image to support the new pattern. Any particular father may need to feel himself in a profound relationship to an archetypal father image if his role is to reflect any deep, positive value on his sense of personal worth.

Al could not find a satisfying deeper image of fatherhood from the family life he had devised with Ellen. He received very little support from the men around him. Ellen was a heroic pioneer to her friends in the women's movement, but Al was merely an anomaly. If he had been more secure, he might have been able to accept the approval of Ellen's friends as support for himself also, but instead he felt that they were in competition with him for Ellen's time and attention. Their dyad, which had survived their earlier social and sexual experimentation, had weakened under the stress of parenthood. Neither of them was prepared to make the truly radical commitments to each other and their children that their "dyadic" parenting required. They gradually retreated into life styles and fantasies that were more familiar and that also excluded each other, until their marriage broke apart.

It has only been in the past few years that men like Al have been able to consciously design a fathering style to include earth as well as sky functions in a relatively equal blend with their partners. It is too early to know what will happen to these families, to see what kind of balance they will achieve in their personal and parental lives. Some have divorced and gone on to new commitments. Others have remained together but gradually returned to more traditional patterns once the experimental fervor has subsided. They are often stronger for these explorations. Just as the sexual experience with other partners before marriage can increase a real commitment to one another by exploding unrealistic fantasies and expectations, so, too, trying out an innovative parenting style before settling on the traditional ones can strengthen a family. Both partners learn what they need to do, not what society or family or friends imply they should do. Couples who risk experimentation at the beginning at least create the possibility of arriving at mutually satisfying patterns.

Many committed parents do not know what to do with the choices that are now available to them. Perhaps they are afraid of the responsibility involved in deciding for themselves what kind of parent to be. We all grasp desperately at rules, regulations, and even limitations on freedom. Fathers do not usually see themselves as escaping freedom or even as making choices about how to be a father when they take on an extra job or strive to advance their careers. It is usually thought of as a matter of economic necessity, of external circumstance rather than internal need. The men who take on more work—and the wives who encourage them—are choosing (or at least accepting) the time-honored role of economic provider, of sky parent, for the father. With this choice, they are also excluding all other styles of parenting—perhaps even one that would be more congenial with their temperament.

If there are few images from the historic or mythical past for the earth father, there are even fewer in our present society. On a personal level, a man who tries to continue as nurturant parent is almost always confronted by more than the void created by the absence of any earth father in his own childhood. He may also confront a void among his peers, who he thought were struggling with conflicts like his own. One father, Mark, describes his own struggle to know what to do with his involvement as dyadic parent and as an earth father:

> *Marcy told me to tell you that I do a lot of mothering, too; and I do. I think what she meant was I do a lot of hugging and snuggling. But it's not always easy. My biggest problem related to fathering is that my image is that a father should be perfect. There are times when I feel inadequate—not all the time, but there are times when I*

feel like I should handle it better. And it seems as though other men, other fathers, don't have this problem.

Once I was sitting in a car with a group returning from playing basketball. There were four of us in the car and what I said was, "Hey, you guys are all fathers. I'm having a problem. The problem is, I'm in constant conflict with my kid and I don't know what to do. You know, what happens when there is a battle between you and your kid? You know, you guys? Anybody got an answer? What happens, do you know—do they outgrow it or what?" That's what I asked. Whoo. Nobody said anything. And I, uh, I said to myself, "Okay, so nobody's going to help."

All along, from the time Joey was born, I pretended I knew what to do, how to do it. I didn't know. I never touched a baby in my life. I just bluffed my way through. But Marcy didn't know much either, so she thought I was good at it. But I have this problem with feeling guilty all the time. A father has to do everything, you see. He has to play ball, take his son for a walk, has to be a stereotype father, to be caring and considerate, fair, listen to problems, to be perfect. All my life I spent a lot of time imagining what it would be like to be a father. When I have problems is when I don't live up to it, when I fail in my image and feel inadequate. Every morning I would wake up and go in to him and he'd goo goo, ga ga, and we'd play, but I wanted it always to be perfect. I was asking more of myself than I could give.

But you know, I have gone this far in my fathering, and it's pretty neat. My father died when I was four and look at me, look at all the wonderful things I've seen and all the pleasures and all the joys that I've had with my kids. I'm a nurturant man. I've been lucky. I work out my schedule so that when the kids come home, I'm home. I may be reading a newspaper, but I'm around. We do all our problem solving together, and we're close. But I've had to work at it. Sometimes I feel like I'm the only man in the world struggling with these problems.

Mark's description of his inability to involve his male friends in the intimacies of fathering (as distinct from investments, trusts, college fees—sky father things) is typical of the way in which the earth part of fathering is still isolated from mainstream parenting, still perceived as unmanly.

Men like Mark feel as though they have nowhere to turn. When Mark did not get any support from his friends on the outside, he looked inside himself. Through introspection, some therapy, and a lot of guts, he found a way towards a style he is becoming proud of.

As Mark says, he was lucky. Professionals cannot always help. Many of them, men and women, are caught up in an acceptance of a subtle downgrading of the father's family role, a bias which inevitably enters into the helping context. As Mark found out, other men are hard to talk with about parenting. They find work and sports and women more "relevant" topics. Even in men's groups and books on male psychology, this aspect of fathering receives far less discussion than more popular issues of men's liberation. Men seem to have as much difficulty talking about successful, joyful fathering as about their sense of discouragement or failure in the role. Mark was lucky to have a wife who helped him, but the real factor was the personal courage he showed in pursuing the deep inner need to be a good father.

Because the earth father image is so seldom allowed to develop as part of a male personality, an American father who does make the choice to be actively and nontraditionally involved in parenting, particularly of infants or young children, may find he has to make some unexpected changes in his life style. While girls usually grow up assuming that they should plan their future in a way that accommodates for family life, especially for the care of children, boys receive no such training. They expect to work harder outside the home to provide for the family. It rarely occurs to them to limit their career,

even for a few months, in order to care for their baby, and yet
that is precisely the orientation that an earth father requires.

David Steinberg wrote a journal during his transition into
the role of father. He was working on his personal attempt to
redefine fatherhood. As every man finds, that effort also required a redefinition of his own life:

> *After six months I'm finally letting go of my old life for
> the new one that includes Dylan [his son]. I see now that
> my old life is really gone and that the job is to build a
> new one that I like as well or better. Letting go means
> that my energy can go into building instead of mourning
> what had died. One day, I cried at the ocean, saying
> goodbye to a life that I loved and had worked hard to
> create.*[1]

A father ought to be able to let go of his old life and embrace
the new identity of father, but how is he going to know what
the new life will be? Who will be his models, who will show
him the possibilities of his new life? Even if he has been
involved in the pregnancy and the birth, what can he integrate
from that experience as an ongoing style? Of all the images
and styles of fathering, the earth father is the hardest to express
in the real world of the family.

When we discovered men who were successfully living out
this form, there was often a special circumstance which, in
their minds, had made it possible or necessary. For Mark, it
was his father's early and sudden death and the need to give
his children what he had missed. A wife may be the higher
wage earner, so the husband may be economically forced to
stay home with the children. Or, the death of a wife or the
dissolution of a marriage may leave a man as the sole custodian
of his children.

When men are finally alone and responsible for their chil-

---

[1]David Steinberg, *Fatherjournal: Five Years of Awakening to Fatherhood.*
Albion, California: Times Change Press, 1977, p. 17. Copyright © 1977 by
David Steinberg.

dren, a new side of parenting can emerge. A man we will call Jerry described his experience after taking his wife to the airport for a trial separation.

We [he and his son] were driving along the coast. The view was breathtaking. I liked the feeling of my son sitting beside me. I stopped the car and took him by the hand as we walked up the spine of a short hill to better appreciate the view of land and ocean. As I stood on top of the hill with him, gazing down at the water, I felt a strong surge of responsibility to him. It felt right. I felt a sense of completeness that was new to me. I felt full, a gut experience. It wasn't a sense of going beyond myself. Just a knowing that it was good. A rightness.

Jerry felt that he first really became a father while standing on that high hill. Once he had his boy alone, he felt committed to active parenting for the first time. He realized that his little boy was going to need a lot of attention, but he felt that he, the father, could provide it all.

Jerry did, in fact, become a royal father, for he never developed an ability to stay engaged in earth parenting while his wife was with him. She returned from the trial separation but soon left again, permanently. Jerry became the custodial parent, not only of his first child, but also of the children he had with his second wife, whom he also divorced. He was amazed to discover that parenting was one of the most important forces of his life. He felt that he had created this part of himself from a void, for his own father had been a weak and demeaned figure in his life. He relished his own indisputable importance to his children.

Because of the extent to which masculine values stress success in the outside world, the father who remains at home even part-time as an earth parent may consider himself a failure. If he is home because he is unemployed or discouraged, he may suffer from feelings of self-reproach and low self-esteem and either retreat within himself or become arbitrarily authoritarian. He may become resentful of a working wife or a maturing son who threatens to become more successful than he in the outside world. Such a father is likely to appear involved in all the details of family life and yet gain little respect and no sense of paternal worth from his family. Sky father and earth father war within him, giving him no peace.

Our world still has trouble accepting the idea of a man being a house-husband by choice. When a man quits work to stay home, people will ask, What are you *really?*, searching for a category like "inventor" or "writer" or "lawyer." Some men who do not want to accept the social stigma of being a house-husband use their wives as a cover for their own desire to be an earth parent. It may take years for them to recognize that it is really they themselves who want to be nurturant. A "closet" earth father is like a "closet" homosexual; in both cases the social stigma prevents a wholehearted commitment to a genuine identity. A father may find himself struggling to replace his wife in the home, just as a wife may struggle with her "unacceptable" need to leave her children to someone else's care and renounce "motherhood" in its conventional sense and find another more satisfying activity. It is not uncommon for a couple to have such fantasies mesh; both may be unconsciously attracted to the hidden desires of the other, and yet the weight of convention keeps him in his sky position and her in her earth roles. If a relationship has a great deal of trust and positive regard, these tendencies can gradually be developed during the parenting years until both individuals are parenting in the way that suits them best.

Some couples shift gradually from traditional to dyadic parenting as they recognize their complementary skills and their mutual desire to share as much as possible of their lives together. It often comes as a surprise that the male is the more nurturant parent or the female the one who is more interested in the sky world.

Aaron is a father who had not recognized his own potential for being an earth parent until he had already been a father for several years. As his second child was moving out of diapers, he realized that he had missed out on his children's infancies. It suddenly occurred to him that he didn't have to be confined by the roles he thought belonged to fathers; he could do anything he wanted; he could go beyond the things his own father had done. Like Mark, quoted above, he had already demonstrated success in the work world. Why not try out parenting as a career?

> *I realized I had missed the intimate experience with the kids when they were little, like telling stories, talking to them as long as they wanted at bedtime, being there at lunch, helping them tie their shoes, teaching them to read. I knew that Donna could do these things for them just as my mother had done them for me, but I wanted to have the experience. I was the primary wage earner, but Donna was working part-time and was earning more money each year. I realized that I could work less and we'd still have enough money to live on. So I did it. I became so involved with the kids that they started to call me Mommy some of the time. Donna was moving outside more, and they sometimes called her Daddy.*

As this family developed, Aaron continued to develop as an earth parent as Donna became the primary wage earner and he stayed at home more with the children. They learned to expect him to be there when they came back from school, and they expected her to arrive for supper.

Even with today's changing roles for women, men who want to play such an important role in their children's lives will rarely find a wife so willing to become a sky mother. Perhaps it will take many generations of "liberated women" to produce daughters who do not see the family as their territory even when they are not at home any more than the men. A woman may be overjoyed to find that her husband is a nurturant caregiver at first, but she often conceptualizes his nurturant activity as supporting her mothering rather than seriously competing for the primary parenting role. In pure form, an earth father requires a sky mother. Few women are able to accept that role fully without guilt or competitive outbursts. One working woman told us she would rather hire a housekeeper than allow her husband to become central to her children. She wanted to work, but she thought of the children as "hers," not "theirs." A housekeeper could not threaten that fantasy. A father who added actual caretaking to his legal and biological claims would force upon her the knowledge that no one can claim a full outside identity without losing something as a parent. Not every wife is like Donna.

Perhaps the most common cause for the shift from traditional sky fathering to earth fathering is divorce. Mothers still usually gain the primary responsibility for their children, but there seem to be an increasing number of custody battles that are won by the fathers. Because of his interest in fathering, Arthur has occasionally been asked to be an expert witness when a man is demanding the right to be legally recognized as the better parent to care for the children after a divorce. A first step in such cases is to confront both parents, but particularly the father, with the facts of earth parenting. Many men shrink away from the job when they appreciate fully what would be required of them were they to gain custody. As one put it, "Even screwing the hell out of my ex is not worth that." In other words, he was seeking custody to defeat his wife rather than from a deeper desire to care for the children. But there are men who genuinely want to take on the nurturant functions for their children. They are too often ignored, though today's courts are increasingly more inclined to give them a hearing. For some, a custodial pattern of three days with one parent and four with the other allows both father and mother to remain in close contact with the children as earth parents. When the father is allowed only one day a week or every other weekend with his children, he may have trouble maintaining the comfortable flow of intimate parenting.

When men gain custody of their children, it sometimes takes them months to appreciate their own nurturant capabilities. The tendency is often to assume that they must find a new "mother" for the children either by finding a full-time housekeeper or by acquiring a new wife as soon as possible. Old assumptions die hard, but many men have learned—to their amazement—that they are more competent and nurturant than any of the women they had been counting on before.

Consider the story of Steven, a father who gained custody of his children after long years of conflict in his marriage, and who required years of a very gradual and chaotic process to discover that he was the better earth parent. He describes his initial assumptions about parenting in the marriage and about his wife Julie.

My feeling about her job as a parent had to do with my feeling "I don't know what parenting is about and you probably do." I was sure there was some difference in the female role; I was certainly satisfied with what she was doing. If there were any disagreements over the care of our first baby, I just asked her advice or did what she said unless I had some solid ground. Now, looking back, I don't think that she knew much or had any experience. Worse than that. Most people don't know much when they start, but I don't think she had good feelings, good sensibilities about what to do. I didn't develop any super pride in taking care of the kids or in fathering particularly. Well, I don't know, I did have some, but I guess after the break-up it became something special that I had to prove I could do it alone. You know, do all the things that a female or a male could do.

My feeling later, when we had two, was that she just didn't even want to be bothered with any of it. She didn't like doing it. Mothering was not her thing, and she often said that. Why didn't I believe her earlier? There was one traditional thing that she did and that was a meal a day, but a good part of the time that we were together there was a live-in housekeeper and a live-out babysitter. Under these conditions, it seemed unclear to hear those complaints about "I'm tired of all this mothering."

Finally she made arrangements to go up to Maine for a week to "get her head straightened out." She took the kids. She ended up staying two months and then writing a letter saying she wasn't coming back. Well, at that point I threw my sleeping bag in my truck and went up there to bring them all back. As it turned out, she was shacked up, literally in a shack, with a guy. The kids were on their own. Julie gave them two dollars a week to babysit themselves!

When I arrived, the kids just clung to me. They all were scared to death because they had been alone so much, especially at night. Billy, who was eight, was supposedly in charge of the others, who were three and four. They were all in this open-up sofa bed in this one-room shack in a more or less strange place.

I brought them all back. Within two weeks Julie was gone again. She left the kids with me that time. It was supposed to be just for the weekend, but it got extended.

After a week she called, and I said, "Well, obviously you don't want to come back. Why don't you just stay there with this guy and get things straightened out. I'll take care of everything down here, it's apparent to me that you're not stable enough to take care of the kids."

Up until then, I had assumed that I had to be the one to move out. It's the male role. The men all move out. It's like bowing, it's the polite thing to do. It's a male thing not to cause hardship on a woman. He drives the car and opens the door and moves out rather than having her make those arrangements. In a way, it's more a matter of "polity" than anything else.

Even then, I was willing to let her have custody as long as she stayed within an easy drive of me. She had been taking LSD and all kinds of stuff, and that really bothered me. Billy had been drunk—the people she was with told me this. They were a hell of a lot more responsible than she was, and they would sort of sneak the opinion that I really ought to straighten things out there. I just knew that I couldn't be that far away any more.

Then a lawyer advised her that I should be the one to move out of the house and that she should come back and get the children, or else she would jeopardize her right to custody and child support. I got mad—and afraid. I told the lawyer on the phone that when she gets home there will be no children here, and I'll move out on those terms, and I'll see you in the courtroom and let the court decide. So I packed them up and put them in the truck. I was very frightened that she and her boyfriend might show up before I got out and that we'd have a brawl. Then I went into hiding with all three.

Despite the extreme provocation by his wife, Steven denied his capability to become a primary caretaker. It simply did not fit his social image of fatherhood or of motherhood, even when he had actually been handling the job. The "male role" was to be sky father, to move out if that was what it took to allow the woman to be comfortable. He assumed that his wife should be the one who would know more about children, while he should be the wage earner. In fact, she earned no money, but neither did she prove to be very nurturant. It took him four and a half years to realize that he was better equipped than she to take care of the children. He was helped in his discovery by his wife's rather overt rejection of her mothering role.

Like many men who have a sense of mission about taking care of children, Steven had had a cold and abusive father whom he hated. He wanted to save others from a childhood as bad as his own, but he thought the savior had to be the mother. The irony is that Steven was always nurturant. From his teen years, he was actively involved in social issues and was a "big brother" to the neighborhood children. He married only so that he could have children of his own; if he had had a clearer image of the possibilities of himself as earth father, he might not have had to go through the long internal struggle it took to get him past his "polity."

Since taking over on his own, Steven has become a royal father rather than an earth father; he continues to be the provider and community link while also being the only nurturer in his family. He admits that he is a good administrator. He thinks that is the most important skill for managing a household—he runs it the way he would run an office or a summer camp. However, when there is a conflict between professional opportunity and family, his work always takes second place. He has neither the time nor the inclination to take business trips or to attend professional meetings at night. He takes the time away from domestic matters only to earn the money he needs to stay ahead of welfare. He does use babysitters to get time off, and he dates occasionally, but he does not need a "mother" to take care of his brood. He describes a three-day stretch when he and all three kids came down with the flu. They dragged their sleeping bags and pillows into the living room and lived on hot soup and orange juice in front of the TV. If a fairy godmother had come along with an armful of vaporizers and scrubbed them all soundly and put them to bed, he would have had the luxury of being taken care of for a change. He wouldn't mind that. But as he says, he doesn't "take care of" the kids because it is easy.

Steven, like Aaron, had the talent and desire for earth parenting. He did not have Aaron's good fortune to work out a dyadic blend of sky and earth with his wife. For him, the only solution was to do it alone, as a royal father.

Steven's was an extreme solution, but appropriate under the circumstances. It has now been six years since he took over as a royal parent, and it is unlikely that he will share his authority with a partner. As is so often the case, the extreme idealization of mothers which blurred his vision of Julie for so long is paired with an equally profound distrust of women. He can't help feeling that any woman might become another Julie.

Steven began his parenting career as a sky father, thereby separating himself from any responsibility for the nurturant aspects of parenting. If Julie had been suited to being an earth mother, Steven might never have used his nurturant talents in his family. As things turned out, he became a royal father, able to do both. The common thread in his parenting so far is the inability to share the parenting process within a close personal relationship. He was not able to achieve a pattern of dyadic parenting because the dyadic model relies on a close and trusting relationship between the two parents.

Many young couples who want deep satisfaction from family life take up the challenge of integrating parenting in their relationship with each other. They are eager to see themselves as equals and to strive to be free from traditional sex-linked stereotypes. Above all, they want their relationship to be enriched by parenting. They do not want to lose the romance that had been between them.

Marriage often represents the hope of living out a vision of love and intimacy, a commitment to deep relationships, openness, and fidelity. Parenting may present the most formidable obstacle to fulfilling that dream. A couple may be able to share success, failure, sex, even money and friendship, but find unexpected areas of conflict when it comes to raising a child. There have always been some couples who have succeeded in staying close, intimate, and understanding with each other, even through the role splits that characteristically take place during the child rearing years. Now that parenting styles and sex-role behavior are coming under question, as men are thinking about nurturance and women are thinking about career advancement, more and more couples are embracing child-raising as one more activity to be shared. And these couples should no longer feel isolated and unique. Increasingly, dyadic parenting should become a practical and acceptable arrangement. To work on deep, intrapsychic levels, dyadic parenting needs myths, images and legends, gods and goddesses, sacred couples, androgynous images—it needs support on an unconscious level as well as on a conscious level.

When two people must work together as one, it is not easy to synchronize decisions, balance schedules, agree on tactics, and share benefits. In parenting this may seem especially complicated, because it touches emotions and attitudes that were established in childhood and may not be within reach of conscious thought. These unconscious assumptions may affect the way a man and a woman relate to each other as parents very differently than they affect the way they relate to each other as lovers or as husband and wife. Girls are more likely to have been socialized to expect parenting to be a marital and a life task than boys; therefore, the experience of the dyadic parent is likely to be more radical for the men.

There have always been women who both worked and parented. The combination is more rare among men. A man must first value his potential as an earth father. Then he must take that part of himself and integrate it with his image of himself as a sky figure. The attempt may make him feel vague and ill-defined for a time, but he must realize that this is a necessary step toward the goal of becoming more integrated and whole.

Some men begin their involvement with their children in an isolated area, but find that this contact only whets their appetites. They may find themselves taking more and more pleasure in an ever-increasing range of daily activities. A sensitive wife can support this shift by allowing her husband more room to nurture, while taking on more outside responsibility for herself. Such gradual changes tend to be more stable than sudden shifts to accommodate a social movement or a life crisis.

One of the fathers we interviewed chose special areas for intense contact with his children even while experiencing ambivalence about close involvement. Marvin, son of an earth father he describes in Chapter 13, is himself the father of two young children. He is currently a very successful college professor who spends a great deal of his time at conferences and committee meetings away from home. Superficially, he seems like a typical sky father. He rationalizes that his continued success is based on his attendance at these affairs, but he also recognizes that his trips away from home are important breathers for him. When he is at home, he often wants to escape from his children. He uses his den as his private space which they are not allowed to enter. He lives in a university town and has many "legitimate" reasons for leaving the house. He is aware that he is not running away from his wife but from his children.

This description does not sound like a dyadic father, but Marvin's deep links with his family are reflected in the fact that, every time he goes away from home, he has a recurrent nightmare that his youngest child, a daughter, is lost or being hurt in his absence. He often calls to reassure himself, feeling foolish as he does and eager to hang up as soon as he hears her voice. Actually, Marvin is intensely, personally involved with certain aspects of his children's upbringing. He thinks that it is very important for them to be what he calls "juicy people." He wants them to enjoy music and to know how "delicious" sounds and rhythms can be. He personally enjoys physical intimacy and music and is always conscious of these potentials in his children. He works to assure the development of their sensual side. He rolls with them, touches them, plays with them. His behavior is not really sexual or seductive; rather, it is sensual, close, and warm. He is worried about the possibility of taking away his daughter's sexuality by attaching her to him too strongly.

I may have to withhold the romantic, "man" part of me from her. It might hurt her, stop her from becoming involved with others. What I want to do is involve her physically as a person. I want her to know that bodies feel good. The strictly sexual part will come later on, if she's got the good feeling about physical intimacy.

Marvin is never naked around his daughter. When she was five, she had seemed frightened of his penis. He decided that staying clothed would make it easier for her to be close with him and remain unafraid. His physical relationship with his son is similar but rougher and rowdier. But he tries to teach him about gentleness and tenderness, too.

Marvin has taken charge of the musical education of his children. He knows their favorite songs and tries to bring home other songs they'll like. He teaches them how to listen, what to listen for. He moves to the music in front of them and tries to get them to do the same. Whenever he puts a record on, he invites them to listen, to dance, to participate in it with him.

He feels this is connected to teaching them how to be "juicy."

Marvin's wife Linda takes care of most of the rest of the parenting, including many of the functions that fathers more traditionally handle. Linda teaches the children about the outside world and coordinates their educative needs. Marvin simply does not want to participate in these things. He feels awkward and jittery with the kids away from home. He feels he doesn't know what a father is supposed to do in such circumstances.

Marvin's involvement with his children is intensely intimate; it is the kind of communication that goes on in breast-feeding and the earliest parent-infant attachments. He only performs the more usual fatherly protector-provider functions because he happens to earn a substantial salary as part of his personal outside identity. He doesn't really think of that as part of his fathering. If he didn't earn money to give to them, Linda would. He isn't interested in providing them with outside status. He is interested in imbuing them with vitality and a sense of the life force.

Marvin was raised by other people's mothers and fathers, in foster homes. Every once in a while, his own father would show up, back from the Army, back from the TB sanitarium, back from a long trip. Those moments were like a miracle for Marvin:

> *I was loved, held, someone I loved was next to me. That was all that counted. No pretenses of being a provider. That wasn't what my father was for. He was my lover.*

When Marvin was adolescent, his father reappeared for good. He remarried and had another family. There were domestic difficulties, fighting, money problems. He saw his father squeezed by the family. He became more real and less romantic:

> *He was eaten alive by them. Sometimes he'd sit me down and tell me about how he deserved more from the family. I'd think, "Fuck you, family," and want to ask him, "Why*

*don't you just be the old way, warm and available? Fuck
all the cares and money problems. Come back to me.''*

Marvin took after his own father. Both of them had a unique,
sensual part of themselves connected to their fathering identities. All the other functions, especially the boundary functions, were unreal and even frightening. Marvin needs to be
with the family, but not to be the head of it.

Linda has accommodated to his unconventional involvement
by taking on more boundary roles than many women. She
handles the finances, does the ordering if the family goes to a
restaurant for dinner, keeps her own career as a social worker
going on a part-time basis and, most important, makes no
demands on Marvin to be the kind of husband and father that
he does not want to be. She enjoys his sensuality and her own
competence. She is domestic and nurturant, performing most
of the traditional earth parent roles, but she is also working on
the boundaries of the family, effective as a sky parent. Thus
Marvin can also be both sky parent and earth parent. His
experience of his father in childhood has been integrated into
his adult sense of himself as a person and as a father—integrated and also transcended, for Marvin's fathering style is
more consistent than his father's. It is also better blended in a
complete atmosphere of trust and security which he and Linda
have achieved together.

One of the important qualities that is necessary for dyadic
parents is the ability to remain flexible in their earth and sky
roles while holding on to the basic assumption that both are
equally committed to the centrality of parenting. Both must be
amenable to a change in the parenting styles of the other. This
flexibility is the essence of syzygy,[2] the conjunction and opposition of two yoked images that are equal though not alike.
If the roles were unchanging, the pattern might become brittle
and lose its vitality.

Some men find that they want to be more involved in the
earth parenting at certain stages of their lives than at others.

---

[2]See the definition of syzygy discussed at length in Chapter 6.

Others become more and more engrossed and get increasingly involved in family affairs. But whenever a shift takes place, whether gradually or suddenly, the mother must accommodate her own roles in order to achieve a new balance. Reciprocally, the father must accommodate to shifts in the mother's style. Like the alchemical syzygy, the pair must achieve a synchrony within the dyad so that each partner gains from the other's development.

A man we will call Paul told us about the changes that occurred in his style of fathering as a result of his son's close brush with death.

I was interested in being a father, but not interested enough to sacrifice an important meeting or a professional opportunity to be with them. I especially did not want to give up time alone with my wife because of the children. It was hard to see what kind of really close role I could have with my two little kids. I loved them. I enjoyed watching them play. I read to them and kissed them good night. I even taught my oldest to read. I was home a lot and I felt identified with my growing family. I was at the head, kept the money coming in, helped with most of the parenting decisions. I wanted my kids to see me as competent and powerful. I loved it when I'd return from a trip and they'd run to greet me, yelling "Daddy." Actually, I was pleased when they cried when I left, as awful as that sounds. It made me feel important. I believe someone looking in would have considered me to be a dedicated father and family man.

Joan was unquestionably the closer parent to both Tanya and Johnnie. I was confident about her ability to understand and care for my children. I rarely felt as connected to my kids' immediate needs as she seemed to be. I had gotten used to seeing my parenting role primarily through supporting her work as a parent. It wasn't that my relationship with the children was not important also; hers seemed more important, at least until they were older. It seemed to me that, by providing financial security for my family through my work and emotional security for her through the aliveness of our relationship, I was being an excellent father. The joyous moments with the kids were dessert, and I thought they would set the stage for developing more intense links when they were older.

I learned much more about fathering after Johnnie got sick, and what I have now is far more meaningful to me. But, even looking back from a new vantage point, I still like the kind of father I was then. It was the best I could find in myself; it was also suited to Joan's needs. I believe that, if I had been able to become more intensely involved with either of the children, I would have run into a great deal of jealousy and resentment. At that time in her life, Joan was relying on parenting for most of her self-esteem. Perhaps she limited my relationship with the children by being so possessive. In any case, all that changed with Johnnie's illness.

He was overwhelmed by a series of colds early in his third year. We were living in a small town then and relied on a friendly G.P. who had always seemed competent. But Johnnie kept losing weight until he was little more than a scarecrow. His ribs stuck out of his chest like sticks. He was light as a feather and terribly helpless. Each time he would get another cold I became more fearful and oppressed. I was unable to work and began leaving as early as I could to be near him. At night I would tiptoe out of bed and sit by his bedside watching him breathe. I began to time my breaths with his, including the occasional breathless periods that are part of normal sleep. As I breathed in unison with him, I felt a strange sense of oneness, a closeness that was unbearable and wonderful at the same time. After a while I knew that I was trying to keep him alive through my breathing.

During that time, Joan took a very different stance than I did. She, too, was afraid, but, unlike me, she reacted by withdrawing from Johnnie. It was easy to understand why. Her mother had died a year before. She still mourned the loss. As a young child, she had watched her sister die of an acute illness over the course of a few weeks. It had horrified her; she still had nightmares about it. She was afraid that Johnnie would die. I believe she assumed he would die, and she was dealing with it before it happened. I continued to support her, hoping she would snap back. Gradually I realized that I had to do more if Johnnie was to survive. Without knowing where I would get the strength, I knew I had to change into a different kind of father.

I had never seen it as my task to go to the doctor for kids' visits. That was part of Joan's work, and I didn't interfere except to keep in touch with what was happening. Joan said that the doctor was doing all he could, that it was just a long string of ordinary colds. He had assured her that Johnnie would get better. I became increasingly uneasy about deferring to her judgment in this area.

Finally I went to the doctor myself. He gave me the same story, promising a quick return to health as soon as the present cold was through. I felt possessed by a need to take a personal hand in bringing my son back to health. I made an appointment at a medical center a hundred miles away and took off from work to take him there. Joan seemed stirred by my effort. She came along with us.

After weeks of tests, Johnnie turned out to have a food allergy that caused his stuffy nose and sneezing and also gave him stomach aches so he wouldn't eat. When we learned what to avoid, his weight shot up dramatically. Within two or three months, he was a different child, energetic and happy as he had been in his first two years.

Johnnie had changed permanently, and so had I in my relationship to myself as a father. I stayed on as primary parent with Johnnie. It was not simply that I spent more time with him than I had before; it was that he acknowledged me as the one to go to when he needed a grown-up, and I would make time always to be available to him. I would tuck him in last at night, and we would have long talks. We were connected as totally as I had ever been with anyone. I was closer with my daughter, too, and Joan, after some anxious moments that I might take it all away from her, seemed pleased about the whole thing.

My parents tell me that I had pneumonia when I was two and had almost died. Perhaps that had something to do with how I reacted to Johnnie's illness. Whatever the reason, it happened. Now one of the children is "mine" and the other is "hers." Of course we both love both children, but the primary allegiance is different.

Paul and Joan still remain divided in their parenting, but their split is now less along particular functions. Rather, they have each taken one child as especially theirs, although they are both good parents to both children. Joan still does not perform many sky functions. The home is unquestionably her realm, not his. Nevertheless, she was able to accommodate to Paul's invasion of "her" business. At first it was because she recognized her own withdrawal during Johnnie's crisis, but eventually she allowed the pattern to continue. In fact, she encouraged it. She claims that Paul has become a better husband and that they have more to share now that both of them are equally involved in parenting. She no longer feels his resentment when she places a child's needs before her own comfort or the chance to be with him. She also feels more free to go away from home and leave the kids with Paul because she knows he won't feel imposed upon and they will be comfortable with him. An R.N., she has started training to be a childbirth preparation instructor. Paul is encouraging her in this. She looks forward to resuming her career full-time as the children get older. She says this will only be possible because of her husband's involvement at home.

Once both father and mother have chosen the dyadic form, have accepted sharing and merger of roles as the way they want to parent, they have not necessarily committed themselves to perfect balance or perfect equality. Generally, dyadic parents pass through phases in which one, then the other, is dominant in a particular function. At best, competence and desire of the partners should motivate the particular blend of parenting. In fact, gender training through normal socialization might still predispose each sex towards greater comfort in traditional behaviors, but this should not remain an unspoken assumption. Both parents should be free to experiment; the equilibrium can shift as needs and interests shift.

The challenge for the pair is how to share each new experience of parenting so that the relationship with each other is expanded and deepened without either partner losing touch with his or her basic commitment to the other in the shared venture. Both have to regard the role of parent as a dyad.

The dyadic parents whom we have studied most closely are ourselves. We are not a dual-career family in the sense that we both have to go off to work early every morning and return late every evening. At present we both have careers that we take very seriously indeed, but we both do a lot of our work at home. We both have flexible hours. Neither of us has a boss or a full-time commitment away from home. Arthur writes half-time at home and, while he also has twenty patient-hours a week, his office is only two blocks from the house, so he does not spend any time commuting and often comes home for an hour in the middle of an afternoon. Libby writes at home half-time and teaches and sees clients away from home about as much. It would be hard for us to say whether we work more or less than the forty hours per week of a usual job, because our hours vary with teaching schedule, patient load, research problems, and stage of development of a book. Sometimes one of us works in a frenzy, around the clock, or goes away for a few days to lecture or consult. We can only do those things when the other is able to free up his or her schedule to be with the children. We frequently turn down invitations which conflict with each other's normal routine as well as those which conflict with important family events.

Although each week has its expectable rhythm, we find that we have many breaks in routine, days that are unexpectedly free and days that are unexpectedly hectic. But we have a fundamental principal—not to make a job commitment until we are sure that the family is covered for that time. And there are certain times that are traditionally reserved for family events. Tuesday nights we almost always go somewhere as a family—for a picnic or to a movie, a restaurant, a park— nothing fancy, but just a family outing. Friday nights we all stay home. Weekends we try to have at least one all-family event. And at least twice a month, we parents go off alone somewhere together, sometimes for a day and sometimes overnight.

All of this sounds very equal, and indeed, over time and with considerable pain and compromise, we have evolved a system that we all (including the children) feel is fair. But we have not done away with traditional sex-role stereotypes which still suit our individual proclivities. Through most of our parenting thus far, Arthur has had more sky involvement than Libby, and Libby has had more earth responsibilities than Arthur. Arthur earns more money; Libby cooks more of the meals. Arthur has often worked until 7 P.M. three days a week. Libby has tried to be in the house when the kids get home from school four days a week. Yet Libby also takes more weekend work than Arthur. We do not know how our children will describe us in any books they may write. They may have their own reasons for stereotyping us—as traditional or as radical. We feel we are dyadic. We think that is because we both know that either of us could do (and often has) all things required of a parent. We both pass back and forth across the boundaries between earth and sky. At times in our marriage, we have reversed roles completely. We have each been royal parent for a short time. We do not feel that we are exactly *alike*, but we feel that we are equals in the power of our parenting and in the depth of meaning that all the parental roles have to us as individuals.

Because this is a book about fathers, we will look more closely at Arthur's roles as father. We feel that he has, over the years, used each of the images of fathers that we have described in this book. There can be no question that he has been an earth father. He is by temperament a nurturant person. He has always been intellectually interested and emotionally involved in the life cycle and in family dynamics. He spends a great deal of his professional life as an earth father in the sky realm, helping others to learn about their relational and emotional lives. These characteristics make it all but inevitable that he would be intimately involved in his own family's process. He helped Libby through all of her labors and was there at all the births. With the first baby, he stayed home and fed the baby breast milk from a bottle during those evenings when Libby was teaching. With both of the other babies, he took off from work to take care of the house and the older children while Libby cared for the newborn. He prepares a certain number of meals per week, oversees a certain amount of the home chores, and is always available for heart-to-heart talks with the children. Before about the age of four, each of the children seemed to prefer to go to Mommy with a cut or bruise. After that, there has been no clear difference or, if anything, a preference for Daddy, whose M.D. gives magic powers to the kisses he places on hurts.

As sky father, Arthur gives the family his name. He has the community status of an M.D. and a professor. He has had periods, especially while he was receiving advanced training in psychiatry, of being the only wage earner and working conventional hours away from home. There is still occasional boundary friction when he comes home from work, because he sometimes gets so involved in the outside world that it is hard for him to pass to the inside, where the other four have established a balance in his absence. He has been well trained in all the traditional male roles and is very successful in the sky world. He has had tempting offers to take on exciting work that would inevitably force him to crystallize his paternal identity as a sky father, but he has usually resisted them for the sake of balance in his personal life and in his family.

Arthur has the opportunity to become a royal father whenever Libby's work as a lecturer or consultant requires her to work out of town for a few days. He has found that he can still take care of sky business while keeping everybody fed and reasonably happy. He has known the pressures of single parenting but has also felt the pleasure of being The One for the kids. Because he has had a lot of experience in both the earth and sky roles, none of the jobs of the royal parent comes as a surprise to him. After childbirth, particularly with the third child, Arthur had to take complete charge of the household, including the care of Libby. It was of great advantage to the entire family that Libby was used to yielding up control of the house and of the children's lives to Arthur. Because he was such an experienced father and already so involved in the children's lives, they accepted the week or so that Libby spent nesting-in with the newborn as natural enough. They were interested in stopping by to see Mommy and the baby, but they did not feel deprived themselves. Libby could devote herself to resting and caring for the infant without worrying about whether or not things were getting taken care of. Arthur was also able to take over for Libby during her long periods of mourning when her parents died. Although the children felt her grief, they were comfortable about turning to their father for much of what she had provided.

The major difficulty in Arthur's cycle of fathering has been the psychological work necessary to make these transitions work. Many of the changes he has made in his fathering style have reflected larger shifts taking place in his personal development and, most of all, within our marriage. We consider ourselves dyadic parents not only because of our commitment to sharing all parental roles in the family, but also because of the depth of our commitment to our relationship with each other. Whenever either of us feels strong internal or external pressure to change, we consider the effects of the changes on our relationship with each other—which includes the parenting roles. Arthur summarizes his own experience.

*At the very time my professional career was accelerating
rapidly, I knew that I wanted to father more. Spending a
year in Jerusalem together with my family and relatively
free of career demands had spoiled me. Before that, I had
been committed to becoming chairman of a department
of psychiatry somewhere. Three years after returning
home to the Bay Area, that goal was very much within
reach. I was teaching at the medical school and at the
department of architecture. I was writing and publishing
professional articles. But somehow it all seemed empty;
I was spending so much of my time teaching other people's
children but didn't get to see my own grow and develop.
Libby seemed to be more able to move in both worlds,
family and work, while I was spending more and more
time away from home, and more was being demanded
from me all the time.*

*I went away to direct a long weekend workshop, and I
had a dream which consisted only of pain. Just the experience of pain and loss. It seemed an exaggerated response to a few days away from home. I took it as a
symbol for the larger pattern of absences from home toward which I seemed pointed. It was a turning point in
my life.*

*It would be dishonest to say that I made the decision to
stop active involvement with any other institutions except
my family simply because I wanted to be more of an earth
father. I was tired of the dullness of bureaucratized education and the limits they placed on me. I thought I could
learn more by writing books and doing psychotherapy.
But I also had a vision of being the kind of man who could
play with his children when they wanted, see them off to
school, be around when they needed me, and still live a
meaningful professional life. On another level I wanted
to be more like Libby, more involved with nurturance and
caring. I knew that the same desire lay behind my interest
in pregnancy, that and wanting to be more creative than*

my body would allow. I also knew that if I allowed myself to be more like her, she would probably want to be more like me.

We had long talks about the effect on both of us at each stage in my disengagement from academia (as we always have had about changes in either of us). At times I was all anxiety over what now feels like typical male silliness. Would she still care for me if I was no longer a prestigious professor? Would she agree to live on a smaller salary? Would she resent my working half-time when "real men" work full-time?

The list of questions went on. Would Libby and I struggle more as parents once I was really in the home as much as she? Would I be able to make any impact on my children? Would they understand what I was doing? Would they think of me as a failure when they got old enough to learn about the prestige of office? All these questions, irrelevant as they sound to me now, were important issues in the family. When one really challenges a sexual stereotype, instead of just playing at it, logic and intelligence fall by the wayside. I'm not sure I would have survived so well in my new multiple roles if my work—psychotherapy and writing—had not gone so well both economically and professionally. I think I used the sky world as a scaffold to help me enter the earth world. It is only lately that I really have been able to blend the two creatively.

Some years after I made my move back into the home, Libby decided to go back to graduate school, to become a psychologist. It was an inevitable development. Once I had begun to share the family responsibility so much more than before, she wanted her sky credentials to be stronger.

It meant that she would be away from the house more and I would need to take over somewhat more of the household responsibilities. The practical changes were really quite small, but I found I was again far more anxious than I should have been. She was challenging me in the sphere I excelled in but was letting go. She was still the mother-nurturer, and now she would be the successful "outsider" as well. I began to feel squeezed out of both family and career roles. Again we talked, long, agonizing arguments, trying to define and redefine our separations and our interconnections. I found I had to recommit myself to her and also to the value of my fatherhood. Not for its reward or for the prestige I could get from friends when I told them I was with my kids so much; I had to dedicate myself to the pleasure of fathering itself, to the energy of the primal earth father who values nurturance, fecundity, and patience. Like the earth fathers of old, I had to let my wife become a part-time warrior and trust that our relationship would hold it all together.

Although we have chosen to work on being dyadic parents, we do not view this form of parenting as a panacea for society's current turmoil around the structure and meaning of family life. The need for continuing consultation and compromise makes it a more complex administrative system than either single (royal) parenting or sky/earth parenting in which the role divisions for father and mother are carefully maintained.

Our own prejudice towards working on dyadic parenting has grown from the commitment that we have made to each other in our relationship. It is also practical for us. There is no way around the fact that children (and other family members) can be intruding, needful people. The intrusions must be dealt with; the needs must be taken care of. It is easier for two to share the responsibility of earning a living than to expect one person to go out there and do it all alone. During phases of our marriage when roles have polarized, there has been a tendency for both of us to feel exploited—a tendency made possible because of fewer shared tasks and less communication of feelings and less intuitive recognition of mood shifts.

We are being selfish when we choose to be dyadic parents, because we both really like children in general and our own three in particular. Neither of us wants to risk estrangement from them. We also both like our work and don't want to give up the ego gratification (not to mention the money) we get from it. Only by being dyadic parents can we both be sure of getting as much earth and sky experience as we feel we need.

For the husband-wife dyad to experience a profound renewal together through the parenting years, each must stay intimately in touch with the other's experience and feel it almost as though it were his or her own. Then each can become more than before, not less. Each may experience an expanded personhood filled with new roles and potentials instead of feeling trapped in stereotyped roles or cut off from the other parent.

It is our personal hope that the image of dyadic parenting will evolve to become an alternate form of personal and parental relating. As women strive toward more and more sky roles, men can strive toward more and more earth roles. Dyadic parenting could become a dominant image for parents in the future. It is still largely untried and experimental. There are not many myths to proclaim it as a pattern, nor folk tales to show it at work. Nevertheless, there are important signs that it is becoming a very real image that will shape the lives of many parents and their children.

13

Implications for the Children

Most adult Americans experienced their fathers as sky parents. Our own fathers (despite their many differences from each other) were both sky fathers of the traditional mode. They defined their primary parenting role as protector and provider and worked hard to perform these functions well.

We both know that they were nurturant individuals, too. Like other children of sky fathers, many of our most treasured memories are of unexpected tender moments with them. We respected their hard work and their struggles to provide material goods for the family, to educate us, and to give us the benefit of a prosperous and safe society. Yet we also resented their aloofness, their distance, and the scarcity of those memorable intimate moments. Thus our feelings toward them contain most of the mixture that we have come to expect from children of sky fathers—admiration and idealization, resentment and anger; the dream of a reconciliation which might close the distance between earth and sky (but which never quite comes).

This is our own simplified variation of the familiar pattern between traditional fathers and their children that we traced in more detail in Part Two of this book. We call it "traditional" to emphasize the possibility of "nontraditional" fathers. Most societies have simply equated "traditional" with "normal." The assumptions about the earth mother/sky father split in family and community life are so deeply ingrained that until recently we had almost lost sight of the possibility of an alternative vision of parenting. The split in parenting has permeated all psychological theories, most particularly those related to human development. The psychology of the child as we now conceive it rests securely (and unconsciously) on an image of earth mothers and sky fathers creating a family milieu for their offspring. This becomes most evident when we see children who were raised in other ways struggling to adjust to societal expectations. From them we hear how the deviations from the "normal" parenting patterns caused them trouble. We learn about mothers who were unloving and uncaring and fathers who couldn't set limits or provide well enough. Or we find out about mothers who were too intrusive and fathers who were overly authoritarian. There are virtually no case histories, no books about disturbed children, which seriously question whether the mother was inadequate as a provider or the father insufficient as a nurturer.

Until quite recently, the father's role in raising the children was simply ignored. He was assumed to be in the outside world making a living. It was hoped that he stayed in contact with his family and did not absent himself entirely from his children. At best, he was a loving support to his wife as she raised the children and a strong male model in the outside world. Even now, when there is more cognizance of the father's importance as a *primary* person for the child, his effect is still explored mainly in terms of variations within the sky father pattern. The questions asked by researchers are: How many minutes (or seconds) does he actually spend with his newborn? Could he take over in case of a family tragedy or a grossly inadequate mother? What are the effects of his being a less-than-firm disciplinarian or less-than-typical male figure to his children? Does his total absence create delinquency?

We believe that children raised in nontraditional family milieus—by sky mothers and earth fathers, by royal parents, by dyadic parents, or by parents of other styles that we have not named—will not be either sicker or healthier than children of more "traditional" homes. Rather, we believe that it is important to each person to be comfortable and creative in the parental roles that he or she takes—or better, *chooses*. But we face the dilemma of ignorance. We know almost nothing of the children of an earth father. How will children fare in a family that has turned traditional sex-linked roles 180 degrees on end? We know even less of children of dyadic parents. How will they develop in a family where traditional boundaries between parents are deliberately blurred? We wonder about the effects of such nontraditional parenting on child development.

We will look at what has happened so far in the small sample of families who have adopted these models. But we do not know much. Perhaps it is just this unknowing that has stopped parents from continuing in newer (and to them more meaningful) ways of parenting. A child is too precious to experiment upon unless one is very sure, but how can one be sure without previous experience? It is important to remember that no parent, traditional or nontraditional, can control his child's fate. The process of raising each child is fundamentally an exploration of the unknown potential in that particular human being.

We recognize the need to fashion a more inclusive theory of child development. The one we have now is a special case suited to families of sky fathers and earth mothers. As long as such a model fits the environment in which most children were raised, as it has for centuries, it suffices. Now we need a more general theory which will prepare parents for the effects of other styles of parenting on their children. We hope that this chapter, fragmentary and speculative as it is, will at least be a beginning.

HAVING AN EARTH FATHER

Fathers and fathering styles do not have a direct and logical effect on the development of men's children. If they did, then extreme sky fathers would produce children who also aspired to be extreme sky fathers. This does not happen automatically. In fact, we have found the opposite often to be true. It can be the sons and daughters of dead or absent fathers (who have disappeared entirely into the inaccessible sky realm) who have the most total vision of an all-giving earth father. James Agee, who lost his own father when he was only five years old, wrote an autobiographical novel, *A Death in the Family*, in which he created a vision of a perfect, nurturant father comforting a child:

> *He screamed for his father.*
> *And now the voices changed. He heard his father draw a deep breath and lock it against his palate, then let it out harshly against the bones in his nose in a long snort of annoyance. He heard the Morris chair creak as his father stood up and he heard sounds from his mother which meant that she was disturbed by his annoyance and that she would see to him, Jay; . . . and his father's voice, somewhat less unkind than the snort and the way he had gotten from his chair but still annoyed, saying, "No, he hollered for me, I'll see to him;" and heard his mastering, tired approach. He was afraid, for he was no longer deeply frightened; he was grateful for the evidence of his tears.*
>
> *The room opened full of gold, his father stooped through the door and closed it quietly; came quietly to the crib. His face was kind.*
>
> *"Wuzza matter?" he asked, teasing gently, his voice at its deepest.*
>
> *"Daddy," the child said thinly. He sucked the phlegm from his nose and swallowed it.*[1]

The father proceeded to ask the boy if he were afraid and to turn a light into all the darkest corners and even to probe under the crib to reassure his son that there was nothing to be afraid of. He found an old teddy bear that the boy hadn't slept with in months and told the boy that it was all right to want to sleep with an old friend from time to time, even if he had almost outgrown him. Sensitive to the boy's fear, the father

---

[1]James Agee, *A Death in the Family*. New York: McDowell, Obolensky, 1956, p. 82. Copyright © 1957 by the James Agee Trust.

stayed by his bed, singing familiar songs and speaking softly, until the boy drifted off to sleep.

Because his father died so early in his life, Agee was able to hold on to the wonderful, loving parts of the man. He saw him as earth father and still had little awareness of his sky aspects. Nevertheless, his description stands out as a vision of the perfect father, a vision which is shared by many people who cannot remember the real man behind the role of father—and some who can.

Can a man who *really* had an earth father maintain such an idealistic vision of a man who is admired for his nurturant qualities?

We talked with Marvin, a man who, like James Agee, remembered his father primarily for his intimate, earthy attributes.

My father was really the center. He was everything, just absolutely everything. And he was really a total delight. That's the overwhelming experience of him in the early years of my life. He's very gentle, very loving, very physical. One of the favorite images I have is of him coming home, walking down the sidewalk. I loved his walk because, you know, it was like a very distinctive walk—it was just delicious. It was just lovely, you know, it almost had an odor to it, it had such character to it. I just loved that, and I used to climb all over him. He used to be lying on the carpet, and one of my favorite pastimes was squeezing blackheads out of his nose. He was just, you know, it was like walruses lying around. He was just very loving.

Marvin's mother, frequently absent during his early years, finally left when he was four; his father became his *only* parent. He lived in a series of foster homes through part of his childhood, but his father was always nearby.

He would sleep in a car outside the house when there was no room for him inside. There's no question in my mind that his major idea was to take care of me. He was loving and nurturing.

Marvin learned about caring and nurturing from his father. He is very comfortable using that part of himself with his own two children. He has become a sensual and available parent in his own right.

There is, however, a drawback. Because he relied on his father so heavily as earth parent, Marvin had trouble with his image of sky parent.

The very qualities that made Marvin's father a wonderful parent in childhood caused pain and confusion in young adulthood, when Marvin was trying to sort out his sexual identity and to find a place for himself in the sky world. Marvin was very aware of the gap between his own family pattern and social norms. He was not sure *he* could become a "real man" or whether his father had been a "real man." Now that they are both adults, Marvin associates his father with all that is regressive and infantile. He sees him as a smothering earth parent. In adolescence and young adulthood, Marvin felt that he could not use his earth father to learn about the sky world. At sixteen, he turned away from activities which his father and he had shared and turned to academics. His teachers became alternative models for him. He became a college professor and entered a sky world his father could not even imagine.

When the father expends his parenting energy creating a loving, secure environment at home and is less interested or effective in linking his family to the outside world, his child, particularly a boy, may resent this lack of outside focus. Marvin took his father's warmth and gentleness deep within himself and used that capacity in his own fathering. But it was a long time before he was able to integrate this earth part of manhood with the sky maleness which he found in society as he struggled to be a man in his own right.

A daughter with an earth father may have difficulties with her sexual identity even though nurturance is so much more supported and adaptive in traditional female roles. Accepting that capacity from a male parent brings problems of its own. The following case history explores one woman's struggles with such a heritage which surfaced soon after entering therapy.

Linda was a twenty-seven-year-old physician whose grandfather and father were both doctors. Her grandmother and her mother had both devoted themselves to raising the children and looking after their homes and husbands. It seemed a traditional family in which Linda had made a conscious choice to identify with the men for their sky attributes. Linda was having trouble devoting herself to her career but did not understand why. Then she had a dream of a woman giving birth to a neuter person. Linda experienced the consciousness of the child as it crawled out through many layers of membranes towards an opening. At the same time, she experienced the consciousness both of the woman giving birth and of a man who was watching. She felt cramps in her pelvis and vagina; she also saw the child emerging from the woman's body.

Of the three figures in the dream, Linda felt most comfortable identifying with the child being born. She felt strangely optimistic about the possibility of being a sexless being. She hoped that therapy could help her be reborn into such a body so she would not have to identify herself as either male or female.

The more she explored her memories and dreams, the more confused Linda became about who had really nurtured her. It became increasingly clear to her that her father had been the more loving parent. His office was in their house. She remembered that he spent many hours with her. Her mother was also at home, but despite her presence, she seemed cold and unavailable most of the time. Linda viewed her father as more compassionate and loving. She chose her profession in an attempt to identify with the sky aspect of her father; in fact, it was primarily his warm, earthy aspect that she desired. She was afraid to identify with her mother because she felt there was nothing there.

Linda had found no way to synthesize male and female, father and mother, or to hold on to her own sexual identity. Unconsciously she accepted her father as providing her with all the love and affection in her early childhood; consciously, he could also lead her out into the world, lead the way to her profession. Even though her mother was in the home, her father had become the only significant parent. Her mother was worse than absent; she was there as a negative image of womanhood.

Both Marvin and Linda are examples of children raised by nurturant fathers. Their troubled adjustments as young adults in part reflect the conflict between their experience in the family and the values of society at large. Moreover, in both cases, there was no positive mothering image to complement the father's earth roles. Marvin's mother left him to his father's care much as the traditional father generally leaves the children to the mother. Linda's mother seemed unequal to the nurturant tasks. In both cases, the fathers took over by default and turned out to have the qualities necessary to be good nurturers for their children. Marvin and Linda would have undoubtedly fared better if their mothers and fathers had worked together to fashion their parenting on competency rather than stereotype right from the beginning. Perhaps it would have meant that both women became total sky mothers; perhaps they could have openly shared both realms with their husbands.

The advantage that both Marvin and Linda had, despite the literal and figurative absence of their mothers, was that their fathers could take over as earth parent and did not relegate them totally to an impersonal caretaker. They both eventually emerged as struggling yet competent and relating adults.

When the father is the primary model for earth functions, both sons and daughters may need to struggle with sexual identity issues, but they should be able to transcend the dominant social model of sex-role stereotype and find their own uniqueness. A child who has had a good earth parent *of either sex* has the advantage of being able to incorporate nurturance into his or her personhood.

HAVING DYADIC PARENTS

The earth part of parenting is sometimes devalued by both individuals in a couple seeking to break with traditional parenting models. Men are far behind women in liberating themselves from stereotypes and, while it is increasingly common for women to reduce their earth involvement in family life, it is still rare for men to compensate by taking on major nurturant roles with their children. In practice, both parents too often become sky parents and relegate nurturance to a less valued person. When this happens, the children may feel that they are not important enough to be the concern of their parents. They may also learn that the earth realm is insignificant compared to the sky realm. Unfortunately, this is often a pattern that develops in families that have two career-oriented parents. Neither the father nor the mother is comfortable as earth parent, yet they do not conceptualize the need to give their children a consistent person that can be their nurturer.

A teenager named Sarah voiced the problem of growing up in a home that had no earth parent. Both her mother and her father worked fourteen hours a day and were impatient with the intrusion of family matters into their attention. Sarah filled the vacuum they had left. She developed into an earth parent for her younger brother and sister. She felt that she knew more about what "the kids" needed than her parents could; she was the one who was there all of the time. Her parents would come home from work and expect to be in charge, but they did not really know what was going on. Sarah knew she was more important in the eyes of her brother and sister, but her parents never acknowledged her authority. The various housekeepers they had had over the years were even less acknowledged than she. Sarah assumed that her parents would be unsympathetic to the children's emotional needs. She resented their intrusions at home. She resented it even more when, after fifteen years of what she saw as their neglect and disinterest, they suddenly expected her to adopt their values in the sky realm by going to their old college. By now she hated the idea of a career. Her parents had not raised her, had not taught her to be like themselves. Her deepest values were not like theirs.

A couple who both spend long hours commuting, working, and socializing in the sky world and return to their child and babysitter for an hour or two at night and a few more on weekends may feel as if they are functioning together to provide for their offspring without sacrificing their outside interests or their relationships. However satisfactory this relationship is to them, it relies on a third person as the earth parent. Occasionally this is openly acknowledged with a grandparent or a "nanny." In the United States, this is often not the case. Instead, a fiction is maintained which only surfaces, as in the case of Sarah, when the sky parents suddenly find their values rejected and their parenting roles under fire.

Parents who are basically sky oriented may feel that hiring someone to provide the nurturant parts of child care is enough. From the child's point of view, however, there is a profound difference between being cuddled, fed, and listened to by one's own parents and by a babysitter whose interest and tenure are always in question. When society supports the pattern, as in the upper-class British system of nannies who raise the children in the nursery or the Israeli kibbutz system of communal child-rearing, the children may experience their parents' distance as appropriate. The entire pattern can be quite stable if the child-care system is an integral and important part of the society, not a hit-and-miss tactic.

To be truly dyadic *as parents*, father and mother must be just as immersed in child care as they are in outside pursuits. Both of them must value and perform earth functions. They may use supplementary caretakers, but only on a limited basis. Mother and father are both primary caretakers; the children perceive them each as a real presence with warm authority in the home. A six-year-old child naively reflected this pattern when she was asked if her father babysat for her while her mother taught night classes. She looked at the questioner in amazement and said, "How can he *babysit?* He's our *Daddy!*"

In our own family, particularly with our last two children, we had the opportunity to observe early child development in a situation where both of us were more or less equally involved in earth and sky roles. One of the things we noticed was that the usual distinction between the words "Mom" and "Dad" broke down compared to when our roles were more tradition-ally defined. Our children began calling Libby "Dad" and

Arthur "Mom," and the youngest one called both of us "Mada" for a long time. It was then that we began to realize how undifferentiated we were in the eyes of our children and tried to formulate a coherent framework to understand their development as children of dyadic parents.

We think that the child of dyadic parents first perceives both parents as nurturant. His primary attachment is to each parent and possibly also to the parental pair. Mother and father will be equally approachable (rather than equally distant, as in the dual-career parenting, or differentially approachable, as in the traditional pattern of earth/sky splitting). Whichever parent is there will be seen as the earth parent in his or her own right, not as a substitute for the other. In practical terms, Arthur never "babysits" for his children so that Libby can have "time out," or vice versa. He is as fully involved in intimate relating as she.

Dyadic parents feel alike to the children for quite a long time. The child does not reserve one set of requests for one parent and another set for the other, except to the extent that he has learned to differentiate between the styles of the two parents as unique individuals. He does not use the earth parent to mediate between himself and the sky parent. Both father and mother are expected to kiss bruises and set limits, cook meals and earn money, change diapers and be absent occasionally. This does not mean that the earth father and earth mother are always interchangeable. Rather, their differences will come less from a different role (sky father versus earth mother, for example) than from their different psychological characteristics, their differences as people.

During the first few years of life, all children pull away from the earth orbit of their parents. The children of dyadic parents will do this in a different way than psychological theory usually suggests. The child will emerge from an initial symbiosis which includes *both parents* as parts of the self. The child may realize his separateness from his parents before he is aware of their differentiation from each other. Thus Ari, our youngest child, was more clear about his "I-ness" and his difference from us than our difference from each other.

Figure 23. Ari's Bears. Each of these small stuffed bears, 1″ and 2½″ respectively, are meant to be clipped to a child's clothing, bedding, etc. When our son Ari was eight years old, he clipped these two bears together and gave them to Arthur as a birthday present. For us they reflect a son's profound acknowledgment of his father's warm and protective intimacy, the nurturant aspects of a nontraditional father.

Instead of identifying father with the sky world and mother with the earth world (or both parents with the sky world and babysitter or child-care unit with the earth world), the child of dyadic parents will perceive that both of his parents go into the sky world as well as take care of him. Instead of identifying father as the outside separator and mother as the inside nurturer, he will distinguish outside and inside by gradually learning that he, like both his parents, can also function in either realm, in his case as part of a union with either parent (or both parents) or by himself. Thus, instead of the sky father's being perceived as breaking the symbiotic bond between mother and child (as in the traditional theory discussed in Chapter 7), the child will feel the bond weakening as he realizes that he is not only a part of the parents but also has his own world to discover. The individuation of childhood will evolve as the child identifies with the different parts of each of his parents and their unit and begins to make these distinctions for himself.

Margaret Mead's description of the Arapesh in *Sex and Temperament* provides an opportunity to observe the effects of dyadic parenting in a society that keeps child-rearing patterns relatively constant. As we previously described, the Arapesh mother and father see themselves as equal participants from the very beginning of the child's life, for they believe that a baby is formed from the combination of the mother's menstrual blood with the father's sperm. The joint participation continues into pregnancy because they believe that the child "is not the product of a moment's passion, but is made by both father and mother, carefully, over time."[2] The parents think of sexual relations at this time as important work that makes, feeds, and shapes a child from the first missed menstruation until the breasts grow to a certain point. From that point, they abstain from intercourse until the baby is weaned at about two years old, although it is required that the husband sleep with the mother and baby. Since both parents are thought to be equally responsible for the well-being of the child, both are equally responsible for abstaining. Intercourse seems to be as taboo for the father as for the mother. This is consistent with the intense involvement of the father throughout the period of pregnancy, birth, and infancy. He is not present at the birth, but he is said to "bear the child." He shares in the care of the newborn and is responsible for bringing things for the baby, such as its bedding. As the baby develops, it is as bound to the father as to the mother, for both parents have taken intimate care of it. Some fathers assume the principal care for the baby.

---

[2] Margaret Mead, *Sex and Temperament*, loc. cit.

Both parents are expected to fast and to perform necessary rites related to birth and infancy.

> *Although the Arapesh generally divide work into that appropriate for men and that appropriate for women, child care is taken to be appropriate for both. The minute day-by-day care of little children, with its routine, its exasperations, its wails of misery that cannot be correctly interpreted, these are as congenial to the Arapesh men as they are to the Arapesh women. And in recognition of the father's initial contribution, if one comments upon a middle-aged man as good-looking, the people answer: "Good-looking? Y-e-s? But you should have seen him before he bore all those children."*[3]

Distinctions are still made between male and female roles in other matters, but not in parenting. An example from our own society suggests something of the personal richness and the problems that a dyadic style of parenting can effect. Amy is a fourteen-year-old girl raised by a mother and father who have tried to become seriously involved earth parents, although their primary focus is probably outside career. She analyzed them in their domestic roles:

> *Dad is more unpredictable. He's the one who will give in if I really want something, but he's also the one who gets mad and yells at me. I can never tell which way he'll go. Even when I was really little, like before I was three, I knew that if I pleaded enough I'd get what I wanted from him. But Mom isn't like that. She's perfectly consistent. If she says no, it's no. Other than that, they are pretty much the same. They both spend the same amount of time with us kids and share the housework. Mom's usually the one to cook dinner, but if she's late getting home from work, Dad does it and she cleans up after. She thinks it's demeaning to do housework, but she is*

---

[3]Ibid., p. 39.

*also a nut about it. Everything always has to be perfectly
neat in the house. I think that's related to her being a
woman. Dad isn't that way as much. Housework isn't
emotional to him but he does as much of it as she does.
The main difference between them as parents, though, is
not what they do as man and woman, but how they react.*

At fourteen, Amy already felt secure in her femininity. She
expected to have a career and was proud that her mother had
shown her a woman could do that, but her primary goal was
to get married and raise a family. She wanted to have a close
relationship like they had. Her only fear was that she might
not be able to find a man like her father who would be as open
to sharing in domestic responsibilities!

We watch our own children wrestle with us as dyadic parents. They regularly tell us that Arthur is more of an earth
father and Libby more of a sky mother than they consider
"normal" or "typical." Consciously, they seem to be proud
of this arrangement. They appreciate our availability at home,
but they are also pleased that we are both more or less successful in the outside world. Our flexibility provides them with
an array of models and a freedom from sex-role stereotypes—
or so we imagine. Both our boys and our girl should be able
to believe that they will grow up to be loving in the home and
competent in the outside world. Nevertheless, we already have
some evidence that, as they move out of the home into the
society at large, the children feel pressure to reduce us to the
old stereotypes, to isolate Arthur comfortably as sky father and
to keep Libby safely contained within the archetype of earth
mother.

Shoshana described her feelings on the subject to Arthur
when she was eleven. They were having a heart-to-heart talk
about whether or not he should accept a month-long consulting
job in England, which would be an exciting professional opportunity for him but would also mean that he would be away
from the family for a longer time than ever before. Arthur was
uncomfortable about leaving. He was afraid it would under-

mine the quality of intimate fathering that he had been working towards for several years. He expected his children to feel similarly. Shoshana had an unexpected reaction.

> When I was younger, maybe four or five, I used to hate it when you went away. I would cry at night when you were gone, and even when you came back it would be different for a while. I couldn't seem to get as close as before. Sometimes I used to wish you weren't so close before you left. If you weren't around so much, playing with us and telling us stories and tucking us in every night, it wouldn't be so painful when you were gone. When I was little, it didn't matter to me where you were going or whether you enjoyed it. I could only think of myself and my brothers and how Mom got more bitchy when you were away. But now I think you should go. I really do. It will be hard on the boys like it was on me because they won't understand why you are going. But I'll be proud of you for being so famous that people want you to come all the way to England to help them. You should do that sort of thing. That's what I want to do when I get older. Travel and be famous and have adventures.

Shoshana is delighted to have her father conform to the larger image of sky father. She is willing to have him gone, to miss him, in order to be able to use him as a link to the outside world. She romanticizes his work and uses it as a model for her own future as an independent adult. She even suggests that it might be easier for her to have him stay in the sky role so that she would not have to deal with his crossing and recrossing the boundaries between earth and sky. And while she is idealizing her father as sky parent, she is simultaneously counting on her mother in the role of earth parent. At thirteen she told Libby that she really liked all the professional activities that her mother was doing. She liked the clothes, the money, the renown. She felt it would make it easier for her to have a successful career, too, without being guilty about outdoing her mother. At the same time, she said, she wanted her Mom to be at home more, as she had been before. She wanted her Mom to get all the breakfasts again and always to be at home after school. She felt that Libby belonged at home, even though she appreciated the value of her working.

It is easy for Shoshana to accept the male outside/female inside split that is so pervasive in myths, books, TV shows, and real lives around her. The reality of our actual pattern seems sometimes to have gotten lost as she strives to get us to conform to her other ideas about what father and mother ought to be like.

We understand that Shoshana sometimes has needs to perceive her parents in traditional sex-role patterns. She wants clarity at a time when she is discovering how she wants to be as a young woman, and she finds our mixture of roles confusing. Yet ideally, since she has a model for both mother and father who function successfully in and out of the home, we hope she will be able to internalize both earth and sky functions in her own development, and we see a great deal of evidence that she is increasingly able to do that for herself.

We have chosen our dyadic style of parenting more because of our own individual and relational needs than for their effects on our children. We have come to believe that our most important input as parents is providing a creative environment for them to call on in their development. At times we worry that our pattern, which could be construed as selfish eccentricity, will cause our children pain. Superficially, life seems easier for children whose parents fall into traditional family roles which are consonant with the world around them. The sex-role assumptions which they model from their parents are also reinforced by their peers and by the media. Daughters learn to identify with mother and expect to become an earth parent; sons identify with father and expect to become a sky parent. It's all so neat. Children whose parents have taken on nontraditional roles may feel confused and frustrated as they emerge from their families. Like Shoshana, they may try to recreate their parents in an image that fits their idea of other people's families. In their fantasies, they may fashion an earth mother for their regressive moments or a sky father to help them resist the helplessness of childhood, even when these images do not fit their family reality.

Children will always struggle against the model of their parents, and it is therefore not surprising how *traditional* the children of nontraditional parents can be. Beyond the issues of rebellion and independence, there is a deeper level of what actually has been learned in their family that can be used as they grow into adulthood. It seems to us that the pain of children whose parents have taught them that both male and female are capable of earth and sky functions is part of their quest for an image for themselves. The pain for children raised in traditional milieus seems far greater. What they trade for simplicity and cultural congruence is silencing the nonconforming parts of themselves, developing only that part of themselves that society finds acceptable. The burdens of that "inner suicide" may not appear until they are much older, perhaps parents themselves, when they feel trapped by the stereotyped lives that they have accepted.

Children of dyadic parents receive a nontraditional impression of the nature of sexual differences; this may cause them problems. But because mother and father both combine the basic earth and sky functions inside and outside the family, the children will not link their own sexual identity with certain stereotyped behaviors in the home. Statements such as "When I grow up I'll be a man and work all day just like my Daddy" or "When I grow up I'll stay home and raise a family just like my Mommy" will be meaningless. Being male will not necessarily be equated with outside status in the work world; being female will not automatically be equated to nurturance and home life. A child will be faced with two parents who combine both functions. As Amy learned, "the main difference between them as parents is not what they do or their sex, but how they react." If they must label one sex as competent and valuable and the other as worthless, the children of dyadic parents will do so because they see their individual parents that way rather than because it is a typical representation of one sex or the other. Ideally, both sexes will be accepted as valuable and wonderful.

The children of dyadic parents should have grown up in an atmosphere in which the masculine and the feminine mutually supplement and fructify one another, where mother and father have united to create the child and an environment that is both stable and dynamic. If the child can internalize a man who is both nurturant and competent and a woman who is both nurturant and competent, gender does not become a limiting, stereotypic aspect of identity. A child with dyadic parents ought to have the best possible chances of transcending sex-role stereotypes and of establishing a satisfying life in the outside world while being able to succeed in intimate relationships and family life.

Perhaps best of all, children of dyadic parents will have the chance to see two adults operating in syzygy with each other. They will learn that opposites are reconcilable, that a dynamic interchange can bring growth, that two parts can produce a whole thing.

Recently our oldest son Jonah, age ten, spontaneously told Arthur what a wonderful father he was. After an initial shiver of emotion, Arthur managed to thank Jonah and ask him why. Jonah answered, "Dad, you've done so much with your life. You're here so much; you have plenty of time to listen to all of us, play with us, help us. But you also are so important in your work with patients and with your books. You've done it all. I hope I can, too."

At such moments it is easier to accept the sin of pride gracefully and to believe that the problems we have selfishly imposed on our children are minor compared to the benefits they will derive. We hope at least we have given them the freedom to search out all the potentials for themselves in both the earth and the sky realms.

Index

223